美国语文

—★ 和小伙伴们在一起 ★

2

[美] 埃德温 · 埃尔德曼◎主编
帕孜丽娅 · 阿力木　等◎译

苏州新闻出版集团
古吴轩出版社

图书在版编目（CIP）数据

美国语文.和小伙伴们在一起/(美)埃德温·埃尔德曼主编；帕孜丽娅·阿力木等译.--苏州：古吴轩出版社，2016.12（2024.9重印）

ISBN 978-7-5546-0789-3

Ⅰ.①美… Ⅱ.①埃… ②帕… Ⅲ.①英语课—小学—美国—教材 Ⅳ.①G624.311

中国版本图书馆CIP数据核字(2016)第248042号

责任编辑：蒋丽华
见习编辑：薛 芳
策　　划：党霄羽
封面设计：沈加坤

书　　名：**美国语文——和小伙伴们在一起**
主　　编：[美]埃德温·埃尔德曼
译　　者：帕孜丽娅·阿力木 等
出版发行：苏州新闻出版集团
古吴轩出版社
地址：苏州市八达街118号苏州新闻大厦30F
电话：0512-65233679　　邮编：215123

出 版 人：王乐飞
印　　刷：天津旭非印刷有限公司
开　　本：690mm×980mm　1/16
印　　张：16.75
版　　次：2016年12月第1版
印　　次：2024年9月第2次印刷
书　　号：ISBN 978-7-5546-0789-3
定　　价：49.80元

推荐序一

李江月

（伊利诺斯大学PHD，湖北省高考作文满分获得者）

我在美国留学的时候，不仅要承担繁重的学习任务，还要传道授业，帮自己的导师们带本科新生。那时候我就经常想，要是有一套全新的教材，难度适中，学生和教师都能在书中获得营养，让来自中国的学生既能学习原汁原味的地道的美式英语，又能对自己所学的专业有所帮助，还能和各个领域的大咖们谈笑风生，打破很多美国人觉得中国人就是书呆子的刻板印象，那该多好啊！

这部千呼万唤始出来的《美国语文》丛书，解决了大家英语学习和教学的需求。每一篇课文都有精美的翻译，译文都做到了信达雅，读起来让人感觉如沐春风，甚至有时候让人感动，让学习英语这个看上去很繁重很枯燥的历程充满了惊喜。

众所周知，英语是不断变化的语言，也许需要每个学习者终身不断地学习。本套书的英文原版，是由常青藤名校校长精编精选，汇集了许多名家的经典之作，所以我们每一位读者，不仅是学生，还包括老师和家长，都能在这样美妙的阅读中感受到自己的进步，得到切切实实的满足感。这些美丽的体验，是市面上一般读物难以给予我们的。

相比很多所谓“高屋建瓴”的语言学著作，这部丛书经历了实践的考验，是一部非常亲民和接地气的青少年读物，也是家长和老师很好的帮手。

很多时候，因为应试教育的需求，同学们不得不死记硬背许多文学大家的作品，但是他们并不理解这些作品。于是，虽然短期内成绩提高了，却在成年后丧失了对文学的爱好和学习的欲望。不论在中国还是美国，总能看到这样令人遗憾的现象。对此，我们觉得很可惜，学习文学本来应该是一种乐趣，而不应该是一种负担。我们希望孩子们开心地学，家长们愉快地陪伴他们学习，老师们欣喜地发现孩子们的进步，而不是扼杀他们的兴趣，阻碍他们进一步追求知识的脚步。

我们知道，很多文学大师虽然不是专门的儿童作家，但是他们并不是没有给孩子写过作品。本套书的一大亮点就是集结了很多大家笔下从未被翻译成汉语的遗珠之作——在各领域专门为孩子创作的作品。通过阅读本套书，孩子们能在书中了解到许多新奇的知识，坐在家里就环游世界，也为未来的学习打下扎实的基础。

本书主编埃德温·埃尔德曼先生，用他的智慧和孜孜不倦的努力，代替了我们在文山书海的盲目搜寻，就像我们的另一双眼睛，带我们遨游浩瀚的书海，获取人类文明的精华。

一言以蔽之，这套丛书是我用过的最好的美国语文学习、教学的教材，既可以用来自学，也可以用到课堂上。特此，我将这部丛书诚挚推荐给大家。让我们一起在《美国语文》的海洋里自由地冲浪吧！

推荐序二

曹海元

（MIT PHD）

迄今为止，阅读一直是我最大的爱好，而在现今残存的记忆里，我最早读到可以真正称得上书的，正是父亲给我的那套页面泛黄的《上下五千年》。我在脑海里至今仍旧清晰地记得那套书的封面，茕茕孑立的烽火台，赭红的城楼，残阳如血。华夏五千年那时而诡谲绵密时而波澜壮阔的历史也随着作者娓娓道来的小故事，奔涌到我充满好奇的内心，溅起了一片片波澜。虽然以我当时的阅历和见识无法理解许多深奥的名词和藏在历史故事背后深刻的道理，但是那套书唤起了我内心对于知识的渴望。阅读让我得以坐上时光机，身临其境般在华夏文明的浩瀚长河中自由穿梭，在我的心中种下了星星之火。正是这些星星点点的火种，照亮了我内心通往知识殿堂的道路，让阅读成了我生命中最大的乐趣，从而造就了我今天这副模样。

《上下五千年》那套书在我如今看来，也许简陋不堪，只是一些历史小故事汇编，但在当年那个懵懂少年看来却已然是通往圣杯的指路明灯。如今这套《美国语文》无论从文章的文学艺术性、选材的宽泛多样性来说，还是从编排的科学合理性上来看，都要遥遥领先。阅读这套书的少年从中可以先领略中世纪灿若星河的文艺复兴，再遇见近现代疾风怒涛般的工业革命；可以先认识一生锋芒毕露最后却功亏一篑的拿破仑，再偶遇始终沉默寡言却在危难之际挽大厦于将倾的华盛顿。从弗吉尼亚的崎岖山岭到欧亚大陆的广袤平原，短短千言却包罗万象、荟萃乾坤，包含了世界历史、地理、博物、人物、传奇、诗歌等领域的精华。

在我看来，如果说《上下五千年》只是星星点点的火苗，那么这套《美国语文》则是那光芒四射的火炬。我想读者尤其是那些处于学习阶段的青少年，必然可以像当年的我那样，从这套书中找到点燃自己心中火种的火焰，照亮通往圣杯的道路。

最后，用我最爱的诗歌《伊萨卡岛》中的一句话来结尾——“当你启程，前往伊萨卡岛时，愿你的道路漫长，充满奇迹，充满发现。”这也是我对所有有幸读到这套丛书的读者的祝福。我想说的就这么多了，希望我无知和浅薄的序言不会让这套书的光芒逊色。

Preface

In selecting the literary matter that goes to make up this reader, constant and earnest care has been taken to glean the brightest and best from writers who have won recognition through the merit of their work. The lessons have been arranged so as to cover the subjects suggested by the best educational authorities. These selections may be classified as follows:

Classic Myth
Nature Study
Fables and Fairy Tales
Legends
Folk-lore
History and Biography
The Bible
Story and Adventure
Poems about the Seasons
Miscellaneous Poems

This reader is based upon the vocabulary of the first reader of the same series, and is carefully graded to follow that book. New words are uniformly placed in word lists at the head of the lesson, so that the pupil who is well drilled on these lists will never meet a word in reading that he does not know and cannot call at sight.

The reader is the best basis for practical language work, and at intervals throughout this book systematic suggestions for language exercises are given. The same suggestions are applicable to numerous lessons, and should not be limited to the single place in which they are found. While no attempt is made, or should be made, to formulate rules, yet the simplest principles of capitalization and punctuation are developed by practice in writing.

Today thoughtful educators very generally hold that it is undesirable to sacrifice space to questions that analyze lessons.

Such questions to be interesting and valuable must vary with the environment and the information of each class, and are easily supplied by teachers. By conforming to modern pedagogy on this point we have been able to gain space which has been utilized to include several stories exactly adapted in vocabulary to the advancement of the class.

At the close of the book will be found brief biographical sketches of some of the prominent authors represented. Other biographies will be found in the higher readers.

The author and publishers acknowledge their

obligations to Messrs. Houghton, Mifflin & Co. for permission to use "The Strongest——Who? or Which?" from "Little Mr. Thimblefinger and His Queer Country", by Joel Chandler Harris, and for the two extracts from the "Second Book of Birds", by Mrs. Olive Thorne Miller; to Messrs. D. C. Heath & Co. for "The Boy, the Bees, and the British", from "Old Time Stories of the Old North State", by Mrs. Lutie Andrews McCorkle; to Messrs. Charles Scribner's Sons for the extract from "Bob", by Sidney Lanier; for "David's Trip to the Moon", from "The Garden behind the Moon", by Howard Pyle; for "Elephants and their Babies", from "The World of the Great Forest", by Paul du Chaillu; to the Frederick A. Stokes Company for "The Snow Baby" from "The Snow Baby", by Josephine Diebitsch Peary.

前 言

在挑选本册书里的文学作品时，我们始终以认真的态度，搜集著名作家最优秀的作品。本册书涉及的主题，都是教育界权威们推荐孩子们阅读的。篇目大致可分为以下几类：

经典神话

关于大自然的研究

寓言和童话

传说

民间故事

历史传说

圣经故事

冒险奇遇和故事

关于四季的诗歌

杂诗

本册书单词以本套书第一册的词汇为基础，循序渐进地提高孩子们的词汇量。每一课的课前照例有生词预习，这样孩子们只要掌握了单词表，就可以避免遇到生词。

在语言运用方面，本书是打基础的最好选择。书中有一些系统的语言学习建议，并配有练习。这些建议适用于大部分篇目，所以不必拘泥于这些建议出现的位置。当然，也无须把规则都当作公式，一些最基本的大写字母、标点符号的使用规则都能在写作中习得。

如今，有想法的教育家们普遍反对在书中花较大篇幅来探讨文本分析问题。

有关文本分析的问题应当有趣且富有意义，需要就不同班级的环境和具体情况进行调整，还要便于老师提问。根据当代教学法的观点，我们可以有足够的空间，用有限的词汇改编故事，来提高同学们的水平。

部分文章后面设有作者简介，这些作者都是很具代表性的杰出作家。这一部分属于课文的附录，因为里面的一些词对儿童来说是超纲词。其他作者的介绍会在后面几册出现。

我们获得了以下作者和出版社的授权，允许我们采用一部分作品。征得霍顿·米夫林公司同意，我们选用了乔尔·钱德勒·哈里斯的《顶针先生与他的奇异王国》一书的篇目《到底谁最厉害？》，另外，我们还选用了奥利弗·索恩·米勒的《鸟的第二本书》中的文章；征得D. C. 黑斯出版社的同意，我们选用了卢蒂亚·安德鲁斯·麦克科尔的《北美的老故事》中的篇目《男孩、蜜蜂和英国人》；征得查尔斯·斯克里布纳出版公司的同意，我们选用了西德尼·拉尼尔的《鲍勃》、霍华德·派尔的《月球背后的花园》中的篇目《大卫的月亮之旅》、保罗·杜·沙吕的《大森林里的世界》中的篇目《大象和她们的象宝宝》、约瑟芬·迪比奇·皮尔里的《雪宝宝》中的篇目弗雷德里克·斯托克斯的《雪宝宝》。

目 录

Chapter 1

Classic Myth | 经典神话

The Golden Fleece(1)

Long ago a little boy and his sister lived in a far-off land. Their father was the king. Their mother had been the queen, but she was dead.

The new queen did not like these children at all. She did not give them enough to eat, and she often made them stay out in the cold.

At last the queen made a plan to get rid of the children. The little boy found out about this, and told his sister.

"Let us run away and hide," he said. " We must go where the queen cannot find us."

"Oh, yes! Let us go at once," said the little sister.

Very soon they were ready to set out. Just then a strange thing happened. A ram came flying down to them from the clouds. This ram was not like other sheep, for he had a fleece of bright gold.

When the children saw him, they were glad. "He has come to help us," they said, "He will take us away, so that the queen cannot find us." Then they climbed up on his back.

The little boy took hold of the ram's horns to keep from falling. The little girl held fast to him.

(*Greek Myth*)

译文

金羊毛（1）

很久以前，有一个小男孩和他的妹妹住在一个遥远的国度。他们的父亲是国王。他们的妈妈是王后，但她已经去世了。

新王后一点也不喜欢这两个孩子。她不给他们充足的食物果腹充饥，还时常让他们饱受寒冷。

最终王后计划除掉这两个孩子，却被小男孩发现了，于是他告诉了他的妹妹。

小男孩对妹妹说："我们逃跑吧，躲起来，躲到一个王后找不到我们的地方。"

"对！我们现在就走！"妹妹说道。

不一会他们就准备好了。正要出发，这时有一件奇怪的事发生了。一头公羊从云上飞到他们面前。这头公羊和其他羊不一样，他的羊毛是金色的。

孩子们看见了，欣喜若狂。"他是来救我们的。"孩子们欢呼道，"他可以把我们带走，这样王后就找不到我们了。"然后他们便爬到了羊背上。

小男孩抓着羊角，免得自己掉下去。小女孩也紧紧地抱着他。

（《希腊神话》）

The Golden Fleece(2)

The ram then flew up into the air. Away, far, far off he flew. He carried the children safely over the land.

Then they came to the sea. There the little sister lost her hold, and fell into the deep water.

The ram could not stop, and there was no way for the little boy to help his sister. The brother was sorry, and cried very hard, but he still held on.

At last they came to land again, and the ram flew down. The little boy got off. He was glad for here the queen could not harm him.

The boy then went to see the king of this country, who gave him a pleasant home.

Not long after this the ram died. Then the boy took the beautiful fleece of gold, and gave it to this king. The king was much pleased with it, and had it hung up on an oak-tree, in the dark woods.

Other kings heard about the fleece, and tried to take it away. So a great dragon was placed under the tree to guard the golden fleece.

(*Greek Myth*)

译文

金羊毛（2）

公羊飞上了天空，越飞越远，越飞越高。他安全地载着孩子们飞离陆地。

接着，他们飞到了海洋上空。小妹妹不小心手一松，掉入了深深的海水中。

公羊没法停下来，小男孩也无能为力。弟弟十分愧疚，哭得很伤心，但他依然紧紧地抓着羊角。

最终公羊降落下来，他们来到一片陆地上。小男孩也从羊身上下来。他十分开心，因为在这里王后就没法伤害他了。

接着，小男孩去觐见这个国家的国王，国王赐给了他一座舒适的大房子。

不久之后，公羊死了。小男孩将美丽的金羊毛进献给了这位国王。国王非常高兴，将它挂在黑暗的树林中的一棵橡树上。

其他国王听说了金羊毛的事，都想将它抢走。于是这位国王命一头巨龙守在树下，守卫金羊毛。

（《希腊神话》）

Arthur and the Sword(1)

预习

anvil /ˈænvɪl/ 铁砧

beside /bɪˈsaɪd/ 在一旁

church /tʃɜːrtʃ/ 教堂

himself /hɪmˈself / 他自己

knew /nuː/ 知道（know的过去式）

knight /naɪt/ 骑士

read /riːd/ 读

sword /sɔːrd/ 剑

young /jʌŋ/ 年轻的

This sword was found in a very strange place. It was sticking in an anvil.

The anvil was on a stone, and the stone was close beside a church. Just how it happened to be there, no one knew.

One day as some men came out of the church, they saw the sword. But it was not there when they went in. Where had it come from?

The men went up to look at the sword. They read these words on the anvil, "If any one can pull this sword out, he shall be the king."

After some days, all the brave knights met to talk about this strange sword out of the anvil, but no one could move it.

"Let us go home," they said, "and try again some other day." So they went away.

Some time after this, all the knights met at a place nearby. But one of them had left his sword at home.

"Arthur, please go home and get my sword for me," this knight said to his young brother.

Arthur went home, but there was no one at home get the sword for him.

"My brother must have a sword," said Arthur to himself. "I saw one in the anvil beside the church. I shall go and get that sword for him."

(Sir Thomas Malory)

译文

亚瑟王和神剑（1）

这把宝剑是在一个很奇怪的地方被发现的——它插在一块铁砧里。

这个铁砧在一块石头上，而这个石头就在教堂旁边。至于它是怎么来的，没有人知道。

有一天，一群人从教堂出来时，看到了这把剑。可他们进教堂的时候，这里明明没有剑，那这把剑是从哪儿来的呢?

于是，这群人走上前去，想一探究竟。他们发现在铁砧上有一行字：拔出此剑者，即成为英格兰国王。

几天后，所有的勇士都在谈论这把奇怪的剑，他们都试着去拔铁砧里的剑，但没有人成功。

“算啦，我们回家吧，过几天再来试试。”有人提议。于是，大家都散了。

又过了几天，所有骑士再次聚到了附近的一个地方。但有一位骑士把剑落在了家里。

“亚瑟，麻烦你回家帮我把剑拿过来。”他对身旁的弟弟说道。

亚瑟便回家帮哥哥取剑，但家里没有人，他进不了门，自然也拿不到剑。

“哥哥必须得有剑。”亚瑟自言自语道，“刚刚我看到教堂旁边的那个铁砧里有一把剑，我要去把那把剑拿给哥哥！”

（托马斯·马洛礼骑士）

Arthur and the Sword(2)

Arthur rode at once to the church. When he came to the stone, he took hold of the sword, and pulled it out. This seemed easy work to him.

Then he carried the sword to his brother. The name of Arthur's brother was Sir Kay.

"This is not my sword, Arthur," said Sir Kay. "Where did you get this one?"

"I took it out of the anvil on the stone," said Arthur. "There was no one at home to give me your sword."

Arthur's brother quickly told their father what had happened. "That is very odd," said their father. "Let us see about this thing."

When they came to the stone, Arthur's father put the sword back where it had been before. Then he tried to pull it out. The sword did not move.

Next Sir Kay tried to pull it out, but the sword stuck fast in the anvil.

"Now, Arthur, it is your turn," said his father.

Arthur grasped the sword. It came right out his hands. He put it back in the anvil, and took it out again and again.

Then all the other knights tried as before to pull out the sword. They could not move it.

When all these men had failed a number of times, they

gave up. They saw that Arthur was the only person that could pull out this strange sword.

"Arthur shall be the king! Arthur shall be the king!" was the cry. The knights agreed to this.

So Arthur was soon made the king, and was ever brave, and wise, and good.

(Sir Thomas Malory)

译文

亚瑟王和神剑（2）

亚瑟立刻骑着马赶向教堂。他来到那块石头前，抓住剑柄，不费吹灰之力，就拔出了那把剑。

于是他把剑拿给了哥哥。他的哥哥是凯爵士。

“这不是我的剑，你从哪儿找来的这把剑？”凯爵士问道。

“我是从那边那个石头上的铁砧里拔出来的。”亚瑟答道，“家里没人，我就没能拿到你的剑。”

亚瑟的哥哥立即把这件事告诉他们的父亲。“这太奇怪了，我们还是过去看看到底是怎么回事吧。”他爸爸听完后说道。

他们来到那块石头跟前，亚瑟的父亲把剑重新插到铁砧里。然后，他再试着去拔剑，可是那把剑纹丝不动。

接着，凯爵士也去拔剑，但那把剑还是紧紧地插在铁砧里。

“好了，亚瑟，现在该你了。”父亲说道。

亚瑟抓起剑，把剑拿到了手上。然后他把剑放回去，再拔出来，再放回去，再拔出来，试了一遍又一遍。

此后，所有其他骑士也试着拔剑，可是依然没有人成功。

所有人都试了一次又一次，但均以失败告终，最后，他们只能放弃。他们这才意识到，亚瑟是唯一能拔出这把奇怪的剑的人。

“亚瑟会成为国王！亚瑟会成为国王！”人群中传来呼声，骑士们都同意这一点。

于是，亚瑟很快就成了英格兰国王——一个永远勇敢、聪明、善良的国王。

（托马斯·马洛礼骑士）

作者简介

托马斯·马洛礼，英国作家，一生中最有名的著作为史诗式传奇《亚瑟王之死》，书中全面收录了亚瑟王圆桌骑士们的传奇故事和追寻圣杯的英雄壮举。

The Three Golden Apples(1)

Long ago there lived a hero by the name of Hercules. He was a very strong and brave man, and did many great deeds.

Over his shoulders he wore the skin of a fierce lion that he had killed. He carried a huge club, and he also had a bow and arrows.

The king once sent Hercules to find three golden apples and bring them back. These apples grew in a fairy garden a long way off.

As Hercules went on his way to the garden, every one that he met told him to return home.

"Go back," the people said. "Even if you reach the garden, the dragon will kill you."

Near a river Hercules stopped to talk with some maidens. They, too, told him about the dragon.

"What is the dragon like?" asked Hercules.

"It has a hundred heads," one girl said, "and is put there to guard the apples."

"Fifty of the heads are always on the watch, while the other fifty sleep," said another.

"I am not afraid," said Hercules. "Now I must go."

When Hercules came to the sea, he saw a great golden bowl tossing on the waves. The bowl was as large as a boat, and floated to the shore.

Hercules climbed into this bowl. Then he spread out his lion skin, and lay down on it to sleep.

A way over the sea floated his boat, but the hero did not awake until the bowl again touched land.

(*Greek Legend*)

译文

三只金苹果（1）

很久以前，有一位名叫赫拉克勒斯的英雄。他是个强壮的勇士，勇敢过人，做过许多伟大的事。

他的肩上，扛着大棒和弓箭，披着毛皮。他曾经杀死了一头凶猛的狮子。

有一次，国王派赫拉克勒斯去找三个金苹果，并将它们带回来。金苹果长在远方的圣园中。

赫拉克勒斯上路了，一路上遇到的人都让他回去。

“回去吧。”人们说，“即使你能走到圣园，也会被那条龙杀死的。”

走到河边，赫拉克勒斯停下脚步，与河边的少女们攀谈。她们也说起了那条龙。

“是什么样子的龙？”赫拉克勒斯问。

“它有一百个脑袋，”一个女孩说，“那条龙就是被派去看守金苹果的。”

“那条龙从不睡觉。它总有五十个脑袋醒着，另外五十个脑袋休息。”另一个女孩说。

“我不怕。”赫拉克勒斯说，“现在我必须去了。”

赫拉克勒斯走到海边，看见一个巨大的金碗在波浪间漂荡。碗大得像条船，渐渐向岸边漂来。

赫拉克勒斯爬进碗里，把肩上的狮子皮铺开，躺在上面睡着了。

像船一样大的金碗漂了出去。赫拉克勒斯一直睡着，直到碗又一次靠岸时才醒来。

（《希腊神话》）

The Three Golden Apples(2)

In a moment Hercules sprang out. “Now I must look for the giant,” he said, “for he will tell me the way.”

“Halloo!” said a voice.

Looking up, Hercules caught sight of the giant. My god, what a huge fellow he was! Truly he was as tall as a mountain. There he stood holding the world on his shoulders, for, you know, that was his work.

“What do you want?” asked the giant.

“I want three golden apples for the king,” said Hercules.

“The dragon will kill you,” said the giant. “Nobody can go to the garden but me, and I have to hold up the world.”

“Let me hold the world,” said Hercules.

This was just what the giant wanted. How glad he was to be free! It was his first rest for a hundred years. He stretched himself and started off.

Ten miles the giant went at a single step. He waded into the sea. Ten miles more and ten miles more, and Hercules could no longer see him.

Soon the world grew heavy on the shoulders of the hero, and he wished for the giant’s return.

The giant was not in any haste. He was finding it very pleasant to be free. But after some time he came in sight.

Hercules was on the watch for him. Sure enough, the

giant had the three golden apples. These he was tossing about twenty miles up into the air and catching as they came down.

Then the giant gave the apples to Hercules, and again took the world on his shoulders. Hercules went back to the palace and laid his gift before the king.

(*Greek Legend*)

译文

三只金苹果（2）

赫拉克勒斯一跃而起。“我得去找巨人，”他说，“要问问他该怎么做。”

“喂！”一个声音响起。

赫拉克勒斯抬起头，看见了巨人。天啊，真是个大家伙！巨人高得像一座山，将世界扛在肩上——这是他的工作。

“你有什么事？”巨人问。

“我要为国王带去三只金苹果。”赫拉克勒斯说。

“那条龙会弄死你的。”巨人说，“除了我之外，没人能去圣园，但我得支撑世界。”

“我来替你支撑世界吧。”赫拉克勒斯说。

这正是巨人希望的：总算自由了！这一百年来，巨人从来没有休息过。现在他舒展了一下筋骨，就上路了。

巨人一步迈出十英里（约十六千米），徒步涉过海洋。他一步步走远，赫拉克勒斯看不见他了。

赫拉克勒斯很快就觉得世界沉甸甸地压在肩上。他希望巨人快些回来。

巨人可不着急，自由的感觉太好了。不过，过了一段时间，他还是回来了。

赫拉克勒斯留心看着巨人。巨人的确拿到了三只金苹果，边走边向空中抛起，苹果在空中飞了二十英里（约三十二千米）高，又落到巨人手里。

巨人把金苹果交给赫拉克勒斯，重新将世界扛回自己肩上。赫拉克勒斯回到国王的宫殿，把金苹果放在了国王面前。

（《希腊神话》）

练习

抄写下列陈述句。

(1) Put on your shoes, Timothy.

(2) Follow just as the arrows lead.

(3) Be always good and gay.

(4) Go back, or you will surely be killed.

这些句子都是请别人去做事的。你还能找到这样的句子吗？也可以自己造一些这样的句子。

Ulysses and the Wind

For ten long years Ulysses and his soldiers had been fighting at Troy. Now the war was over, and they were all going home.

As their home was on an island in the sea, they had to go in boats.

Aeolus, the king of the winds, lived on another island. He kept the winds shut up in a cave, so that they could not do harm by blowing at the wrong time.

Ulysses stopped to see his friend Aeolus. "I should like to have a good wind that will blow our boats straight home," he said.

"With all my heart," said Aeolus, "here is a bag filled with winds. You shall have it, and then you can choose any wind that you please."

Ulysses first chose the west wind, and gayly it blew the boats toward home.

For eight days and nights Ulysses stayed awake to see that all was right. By that time they were in sight of their own island. "Now all is well, and I shall sleep," said Ulysses.

No sooner was Ulysses asleep, than his men got into mischief. They had seen the queer bag. "It must hold treasures," they said, "for Ulysses guards it with so much care."

Then they opened the bag. Out rushed all the winds, and over the sea they flew.

The north wind made a fierce storm, the east wind brought rain, the sea was filled with huge waves, and the poor boats were driven far away.

They were driven so far, that ten years more rolled round before Ulysses reached his island.

By that time all of his men and boats were lost, and a friendly king had to send them home.

(Homer's Iliad, adapted)

译文

尤利西斯与风

尤利西斯率领众士兵攻打特洛伊城已有十年了，如今战争已经停息，希腊将士们纷纷返回家乡。

因为他们的家乡在海中的一座岛屿上，所以他们必须坐船去。

风神埃俄罗斯住在另一座岛上。他把风关在山洞里，避免它们在不合时宜的时候出现。

尤利西斯途中去看望好友埃俄罗斯，告诉他："我想要一阵好风，把我们的船刮到家乡去。"

"奉上我的心意，"埃俄罗斯说，"这里有个锦囊，里面装着风。你拿着它，就可以让风朝你想要的地方吹。"

尤利西斯先选了一阵西风，船儿轻快地朝家的方向驶去。

为了确保一切顺利，尤利西斯八天八夜没有休息。后来，他们已经能看得到家乡的岛屿了，尤利西斯才说："既然一切顺利，那么我也该睡一觉了。"

尤利西斯还没睡多久，他的船员们就开始动歪脑筋了。他们盯上了那个古怪的锦囊。"尤利西斯花这么多心思守着，这里面一定是有财宝。"他们说。

于是他们解开了锦囊，所有的风都呼啸而出，在海面上飞驰。

北风刮起了猛烈的风暴，而东风则唤来了大雨，海面上波涛汹涌，把这艘倒霉的船送到了很远的地方。

他们被送得很远很远，这一来，尤利西斯花了十年都回不到家乡。

正当他的船和所有船员迷失了方向的时候，一位好心的国王出现了，将他们送回了家。

（荷马史诗，有删改）

Peach Prince(1)

预习

choose /tʃuːz/ 选择

dumplings /ˈdʌmplɪŋz/ 饺子；饭团

husband /ˈhʌzbənd/ 丈夫

island /ˈaɪlənd/ 岛屿

monkey /ˈmʌŋki/ 猴子

peach /piːtʃ/ 桃子；桃太郎的名字

prince /prɪns/ 王子

punish /ˈpʌnɪʃ/ 惩罚

treasure /ˈtreʒər/ 宝藏

In a stream one day, a good old woman found a peach floating. She took it home to share with her husband. Just when they were ready to cut two, and out stepped a boy.

The little boy was the Peach Prince. The old man and woman took good care of him, and he grew very strong.

Long before the little boy came, some giants had robbed the old man of his treasures. These they had taken to their island in the sea. Peach Prince made up his mind to punish the giants and get the treasures back.

"Mother," said the Peach Prince to the old woman, "will you please make me some dumplings?"

The dumplings were soon made. The Prince put them into a basket, took his iron club, called his little dog, and started.

As he went along, he met a monkey. "Where are you going, Peach Prince?" asked the monkey.

Peach Prince told him.

"Give me a dumpling, and I will go with you," said the monkey.

Peach Prince gave him a dumpling.

Then they met a bird. "Where are you going, Peach Prince?" asked the bird.

Peach Prince told him.

"Give me a dumpling, and I will go with you," said the bird.

Peach Prince gave him a dumpling. Then the Prince went on with his three friends.

When they came to the shore of the sea, they found a boat big enough for Peach Prince, the dog, and the monkey.

While they got into the boat and rowed to the island, the bird flew ahead to choose a place for them to land.

(Japanese Legend).

译文

桃太郎（1）

有一天，一个善良的老妇人发现，一只桃子漂浮在小溪里。她打算把桃子捡回家后和丈夫一起享用，谁知他们准备切开桃子的时候，里面蹦出来一个小男孩。

这个小男孩就是桃太郎。这对老夫妻对他照料有加，他的身体也越来越结实。

在小男孩到来之前，曾有一些巨人抢走了老人家的财宝，并把财宝带到海中的岛上。桃太郎下定决心讨伐巨人，并夺回财宝。

“妈妈，”桃太郎对老妇人说，“你能为我准备些饭团吗？”

饭团很快就做好了。桃太郎把它们装到篮子里，带着他的铁棒，叫上小狗，就出发了。

走着走着，他碰到了一只猴子。“你要去哪儿，桃太郎？”猴子问。

桃太郎告诉他事情的经过。

“给我一个饭团，我就跟你一起去。”猴子又说。

桃太郎给了他一个饭团。

然后他们又碰到了一只鸟儿，“你要去哪儿，桃太郎？”鸟儿问。

桃太郎把事情经过告诉他。

“给我一个饭团，我就跟你一起去。”鸟儿这么说。

桃太郎给了他一个饭团。于是桃太郎就带着三个小伙伴一起上路了。

当他们到达海边时，他们看到一艘船，这艘船能坐得下桃太郎、小狗和猴子。

于是他们坐上船，划向岛屿，鸟儿则飞在前头，给他们找上岸的地方。

（日本传说）

Peach Prince(2)

预习

ahead /əˈhed/ 在前面

cave /keɪv/ 山洞

coral /ˈkɔːrəl/ 珊瑚

magic /ˈmædʒɪk/ 魔法

pearl /pɜːrl/ 珍珠

scratch /skrætʃ/ 抓挠

splash /splæʃ/ 泼；溅

In a short time the Prince and his little army were at the door of the giant's cave. The giant tried to fight hard, but the dog bit him, the monkey climbed on his back and scratched him, and the bird flew in his face.

Peach Prince beat the giant with his iron club, until the giant begged for his life, and promised to give back the treasures. So the Prince let him off.

The king giant then made all the other giants bring out the treasures. These were a magic coat and hat, gold and silver, coral and pearls, and many other beautiful things.

The giants put the treasures into the boat. Then Peach

Prince and his army rowed away. Splash! Splash! Went their oars.

There stood the old man and woman on the shore, waiting for them. Soon the Peach Prince, the army, and the treasures were safe, for the giant did not dare to come again to the shore.

(Japanese Legend)

译文

桃太郎（2）

不久，桃太郎和他的小军团就到达了巨人洞穴的门口。巨人试图反击，但小狗咬伤了他，猴子爬上他的背抓伤了他，小鸟在他面前飞来飞去。

桃太郎用他的铁棒痛打巨人，直到巨人跪地求饶，并且答应归还财宝，桃太郎才放过他。

巨人是个国王，他让其他巨人拿出了许多宝贝，其中有魔法外套和帽子，金子和银子，珊瑚和珍珠，还有其他很多好东西。

巨人们把这些财宝都装到船里后，桃太郎和他的军团就划船离开了。他们的桨传来阵阵“哗哗”声。

老夫妇正站在岸边等着他。桃太郎、他的军团和那些财宝都安全了，因为巨人再也不敢来海边了。

（日本传说）

Chapter 2

Nature Study | 关于大自然的研究

The Woodpecker

预习

fly /flaɪ/ 飞

hit /hɪt/ 敲打

life /laɪf/ 生活；生命

sound /saʊnd/ 声音

spot /spɑːt/ 点

tapping /ˈtæpɪŋ/ 凿孔

twice /twaɪs/ 两次

woodpecker /ˈwʊdpekər/ 啄木鸟

Very close to me there is a woodpecker on an apple tree. How odd the red spot is on the back of his head! I should like to know why it is there.

The woodpecker is so close to the bark, that I can not see his feet. He looks as if he had on a black coat open in the back.

He is tapping all around the dead limbs. He hardly hits twice in the same place. He is trying to see if there are any worms in the tree.

How fond he is of the bark of trees! All his life long he

keeps tapping and looking at it. How quickly he runs up a limb, or drops down!

Now he goes round and round, and hops from limb to limb. Now with a soft sound of his wings he flies to the next tree.

(Henry D. Thoreau, adapted)

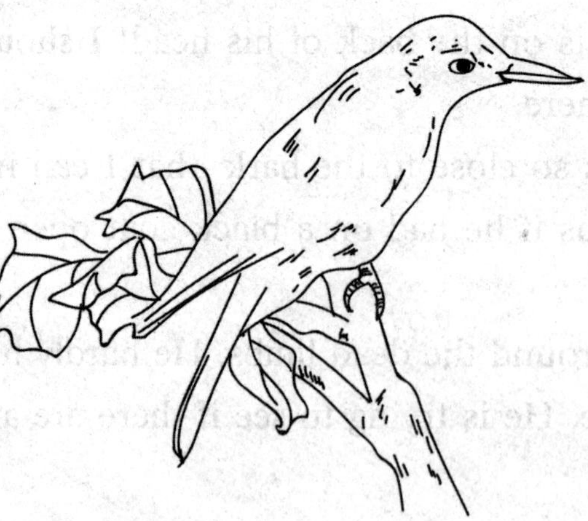

译文

啄木鸟

距离我很近的地方，有一只啄木鸟停在苹果树上。他后脑勺上的红斑点真奇怪！我想知道他为什么在这。

这只啄木鸟离树皮很近，近到我都看不见他的爪子了。他就像穿了一件敞口的黑夹克一样。

他在枯树枝上轻轻地敲来敲去，几乎不在同一个地方敲第二次。他在努力检查这棵树里面有没有虫子。

他多么喜爱这树皮啊！他终其一生，都不断地在树木上凿孔，做检查。他在树枝间上蹿下跳，速度有多快啊！

现在他绕了一圈又一圈，跳了一下又一下。他轻轻地挥着翅膀，又飞向下一棵树啦。

（亨利·戴维·梭罗，有删改）

The Goldfinch

预习

August /ˈɔːgəst/ 八月
canary /kəˈneri/ 金丝雀
goldfish /ˈgoʊldfɪʃ/ 金鱼
lemon /ˈlemən/ 柠檬
mostly /ˈmoʊstli/ 通常地
salad /ˈsæləd/ 沙拉
thistle /ˈθɪsl/ 蓟
weed /wiːd/ 野草

The goldfinch is a beautiful yellow bird. He is of a deep lemon color. His wings, tails, and cap are all black.

The nest that the goldfinch makes is a very pretty one. It has a bed of thistle-down an inch thick for the baby birds to rest upon. This nest may be made as late as August.

Two of these little birds once had their nest in an apple tree. While the mother bird was sitting, her gay little mate stayed near her all the time.

Every littler while the sitting bird would say “S-w-e-e-t” which sounds like a canary.

Then the father bird would call, and fly at once to see if she wanted anything.

These little birds eat mostly the seeds of weeds. They like thistle and ragweed, and seeds that fly.

Often they are called thistle-birds, salad-birds, and such names.

(Olive Thorne Miller, adapted)

译文

金翅雀

金翅雀是一种黄色的鸟儿，很漂亮。他的翅膀、尾巴和头顶是黑色的，除此之外的部分，都呈现出一种深深的柠檬黄。

金翅雀的巢十分美观。幼鸟的床上，要垫一层一英寸（约二点五厘米）厚的蓟。金翅雀筑巢很迟，有时候要到八月才筑巢。

其中，两只幼鸟的巢曾经筑在一棵苹果树上。鸟妈妈坐着的时候，她欢快的小宝贝们就一直待在她身边。

每过一小会儿，坐着的鸟妈妈就会叫道："甜——心——"听起来很像金丝雀的叫声。

然后，鸟爸爸就会一边回应她，一边赶紧飞过来，看看她需要些什么。

幼鸟们大多吃的是野草的种子，他们喜欢吃蓟和豚草的，还有其他可以被风吹起来的种子。

他们通常叫作蓟鸟、沙拉鸟或者类似的名字。

（奥利弗 · 索恩 · 米勒，有删改）

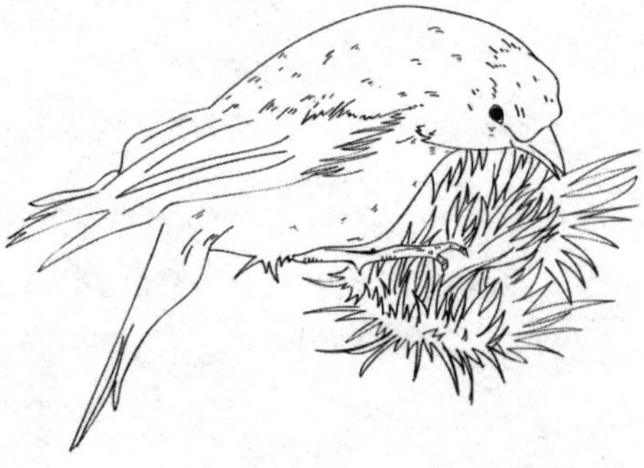

The Cardinal Bird

This beautiful bird has three or four names, but we know him best as the cardinal bird. He lives in all the states of the South, and in some of those of the North.

He is a bright red to the tip of his back. He wears a beautiful crest, and has a black face and throat. His mate has a red beak, and red tints on her dull robe.

Both the cardinal and his wife are singers. He in much the louder, but she has the sweeter song. The poor birds come to harm from their singing, for they are often caught and kept in cages.

While nesting, the cardinals are cross. They are ready to fight any one that touches their nest.

If a snake comes about, all the birds will fly at him with loud cries. They will even fight him if he does not leave.

The nest of these birds is not very high in a tree or bush. They are very shy about it. If it is touched by any one, the birds will nearly always leave it.

Two cardinals once built their nest close to a kitchen

door. They were so used to the people that they were not afraid.

One who lived in that house was a boy fourteen years old. He was so gentle with the birds, that they would even feed their little ones when he was standing beside them.

(Olive Thorne Miller)

译文

北美红雀

这种美丽的鸟有三四种名字，不过我们最熟悉的名字是红雀。红雀栖息于南部各州，北部的一些州也有分布。

雄红雀的背部是亮红色的，脸和喉部则是黑的，羽冠也很漂亮。而雌性红雀的喙是红色的，深色的羽毛上点缀着红色的斑点。

红雀不分雌雄都有一副好歌喉。不过雄红雀的声音较洪亮，雌性的则更为甜美。不过这副好嗓子也给可怜的红雀带来了灾难——人们为了欣赏红雀唱歌，常常把它们抓住关进笼子里。

红雀的脾气很好，但在筑巢的时候，它们会变得暴躁易怒，随时都可能攻击那些接近巢穴的不速之客。

假如一条蛇来到鸟巢附近，所有的红雀都会大声叫着向蛇飞过去，如果蛇还不走，它们甚至会发起攻击。

红雀不会把巢筑在很高的地方，而是会在树丛里或其他安静的地方筑巢。红雀生性害羞，只要有其他动物接触过它们的鸟巢，它们很可能就会搬家离开。

曾经有两只红雀把巢筑在厨房房门附近。它们已经习惯了人类的存在，并不怕人。

这一家有个十四岁的小男孩。他对

这两只鸟倍加呵护，于是这两只鸟不害怕在小男孩面前喂幼鸟。

（奥利芙 · 索恩 · 米勒）

练习

1.写出你家所在地方的名字。

2.给你的爸爸写封信，告诉他关于北美红雀的事情。

3.给你的老师写一封信，跟他讲讲你平常喜欢玩的游戏。

Water Lilies

An Indian camp was close to the lake.

In the day-time the children went out on the lake in their canoes to fish. In the evening they sat on the shore, and looked at the stars dancing on the water.

"I wish that the stars were here in the day-time," said Noco.

A little star heard what Noco said. The star wished to be near the children.

That night the little star dropped from his place in the sky down into the lake.

The star's beams spread out on the water. Here and there they took root.

Up from each root grew a plant with blossoms like the star. They had beautiful white petals.

In the center were yellow stamens like a golden heart.

Then Noco and the other children went out in their canoes to visit the flowers. They were white water lilies, but

the children called them stars.

"Our stars have come to live with us forever," Noco said.

(Indian Legend)

译文

睡莲

湖泊旁边有一个印第安营地。

白天，孩子们乘着小木舟到湖面上去钓鱼。晚上，孩子们就坐在岸边，看着波光粼粼的水面上的那些星星，好像在跳舞一样。

“要是星星们白天也能在这儿跳舞就好了。”诺克说。

一颗小星星听到了诺克的话，想和孩子们更亲近些。

于是这晚，这颗星星离开天空，跳到了湖里。

星星在水中绽放出光芒，遍地生根。

一种花朵像星星一样的植物，从根芽里生长出来，它们有着美丽的白色花瓣。

花瓣中央，那些黄色的花蕊像黄金一般。

于是诺克和他的小伙伴们都乘着他们的小木舟来看这些花。这些花就是白色的睡莲，但是孩子们管它们叫“星星”。

“我们的‘星星’要和我们永远在一起了。”诺克说。

（印度传说）

练习

1. 抄写下列陈述句。

There's no dew left on the daisies and clover,
There's no rain left in heaven;
I've said my "seven times" over and over,
Seven times one are seven.
I am old, so old I can write a letter;
My birthday lessons are done;
The lambs play always, they know no better;
They are only one times one.

(Jean Ingelow)

2. 抄写下列单词与缩写

September....Sept. November....Nov.
October....Oct. December....Dec.

____

____

A Squirrel Talk(1)

"Look! There is a chipmunk, Harry," said his cousin Ned.

A striped squirrel ran along an old log by the side of the road.

"There is an odd thing about the chipmunk," Ned went on. "His hole is as round as if bored by an auger, and there is never a bit of dirt about the mouth."

"What becomes of it all?" asked Harry.

"The hole goes straight down a little way, and then winds off under ground. At the farther end is his nest and winter storehouse.

"You have seen his cheeks stuffed out sometimes, like pockets, full of nuts or corn. That is the way he carries food into his nest. I think that he must bring out the dirt in the same way when he is making the hole."

"There are black squirrels in this country. You have seen them, haven't you?"

"Yes," said Harry. "I once saw a black squirrel eating walnuts. I should think that they would break their teeth sometimes."

Ned laughed, "The squirrels would not thank you if you were to break the nuts for them. Indeed, they have to gnaw, gnaw, all the time, but it is best for them. It keeps their teeth from growing too long.

"If they should stop gnawing for six weeks, their teeth would have grown so long that they could not close their mouths. If you ever catch a squirrel, you will find that his teeth are sharp enough to go through a buckskin glove."

译文

松鼠课堂（1）

“看呐！哈里，那儿有只花栗鼠。”哈里的表兄内德说。

路边，一只有花纹的松鼠沿着一根老树枝跑了过去。

“关于花栗鼠，有一件奇怪的事情。”内德继续说，“他的洞总是像用螺旋钻打出来的一样，但洞口周围一丁点土也没有。”

“那洞里面到底是什么样子啊？”哈里问。

“从洞口进去走不了几步，道路就会盘旋、曲折起来。走到底才能到达他的巢穴和过冬的储藏室。

“有时候你看到他两颊鼓鼓的，像口袋一样，里面装满了坚果和谷物。他就是这样把食物运回巢穴的。我猜他在筑巢的时候，一定也是通过一样的方法来把泥土运走。”

“这地方还有黑松鼠，你见过他们的，不是吗？”

“没错，”哈里说，“我曾经看过黑松鼠吃核桃。有时我还真担心他会不会啃坏牙齿呢。”

内德笑了起来：“你要是去帮他们砸碎核桃，松鼠们可不会感谢你。真的，他们需要反复啃咬，不停地磨牙，才能防止牙齿长得太长。这对于他们来说可是好事儿。”

“如果他们超过六个星期没有磨牙的话，牙齿就会长到他们连嘴都合不上。要是你抓到过松鼠，你就会发现他牙齿尖得很，可以刺穿鹿皮手套。”

A Squirrel Talk(2)

"Ho! There's a gray squirrel, now. See, he has a nut in his mouth. Watch him! Did you ever see one of their nests, Harry?"

"No, I never did."

"They make them of twigs and leaves in the hollow of an old tree, or in the fork of some big trees. There they stay when it is wet, for they like to be dry and clean."

"I saw one in a cage in a store," said Harry.

"It was turning a wheel so fast that one could hardly see it."

"I would not keep a squirrel in a cage. I would have him outside where I could play with him."

"Did you ever catch one?" asked Harry.

"No," said Ned, "but a friend of mine once had two flying squirrels. They were fine little fellows, with beautiful fur of a light-brown color. They had dark stripes on the sides, and were white under."

"Is it true that they can fly?"

"I will tell you about that. Between the legs of this squirrel is a loose fold of skin. When the squirrel wants to pass to another tree, he spreads his four legs, and stretches this skin until he makes himself almost flat.

"He then runs to the top of the tree, and springs into

the air. He does not fly, but with the help of this fold can pass over a great deal more space than he could have jumped across."

"I have seen red squirrels, too," said Harry.

"Yes, they are very pretty," said Ned. "They will take anything that they can lay hold of. They find nuts out here in the woods, and corn at the barn. They steal robins' eggs too, if they can find them."

译文

松鼠课堂（2）

“嚯！现在又来了只灰松鼠。你看，他嘴里叼着个坚果。快看！你见过他们的巢穴吗，哈里？”

“没有，我从来都没见过。”

“他们的巢穴不在老树洞里，就在大树的树杈里，是用树枝和叶子做成的。下雨的时候，他们就会去那儿待着，因为他们喜欢让自己干干爽爽的。”

“我在商店的笼子里也看到过一只。”哈里说，“当时他正在转轮上跑圈，快得都看不清啦。”

“我可不会把松鼠关在笼子里。我会把他们放出来，这样我就可以陪他玩了。”

“你抓到过松鼠吗？”哈里问。

“没。”内德说，“但是我的一个朋友养过两只飞鼠。他们是很好的伙伴，小小的，可爱极了，有一身美丽的、浅棕色毛皮，肚皮是白色的，身体两侧有深色的条纹。”

“他们真的会飞吗？”

“我这就告诉你。这种松鼠的腿之间有一层皮，这层皮平时是折起来的。而当他想要跳到另一棵树上时，就会伸展四肢，把这层皮舒展开，整个身子都快要成一个平面了。

“然后，他就会爬到树顶上，再跃到空中。他并不会飞，但他能利用这层皮滑翔很长一段距离，单凭跳跃他是跳不了这么远的。”

“我还看到过红松鼠。”哈里说。

“嗯，他们长得很好看。”内德说，“他们能摸到什么就拿走什么。他们会找到这片树林里的坚果和谷仓里的玉米。只要他们找得到，连知更鸟的蛋都不会放过。”

练习

抄写下列陈述句

(1)How fond he is of the bark of trees!

(2)Oh, I have it!

找找或自己写些其他表达惊喜、惊异、愉快或痛苦语气的句子。

Bob

预习

hawk /hɔːk/ 鹰

Irish /ˈaɪrɪʃ/ 爱尔兰人

pine /paɪn/ 松树

potato /pəˈteɪtoʊ/ 马铃薯

screaming /ˈskriːmɪŋ/ 尖叫

seacoast /ˈsiːˌkoʊst/ 海岸

spoiled /spɔɪld/ 被宠坏的

thirsty /ˈθɜːrsti/ 口渴的

yolk /joʊk/ 蛋黄

Bob is our mocking-bird. Not that his name should be Bob at all. He should be called Sir Philip Sydney.

Bob fell to us out of the top of a great pine in a small city on the seacoast of Georgia. In this tree lived great numbers of mocking-birds. They love the green leaves and the breezes from the sea, and, most of all, the sunlight.

About three years ago, Bob was lying on the ground in a lump. He was only a few days old. He could not be put back into the tree, for fear a hawk would take him.

His nest was not to be found. So we made a place for him, and took very good care of him.

Soon he began to call for his food as loudly as any spoiled child. When it was brought, he would throw his head back, and open his yellow beak very wide. Then the lady that cared for him would put into it ball after ball of the yolk of egg mixed with Irish potato.

A short time after Bob came to us, another little bird without a home was put into his cage. One day, when Bob was about six weeks old, his breakfast was late. He was hungry, indeed, and was screaming with all his might.

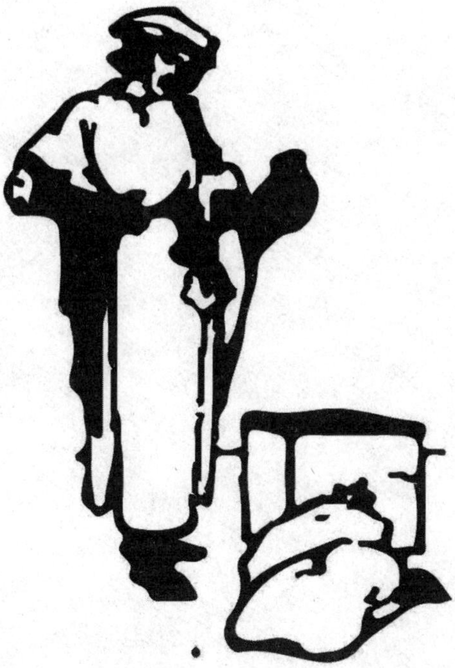

At last the lady of the house was able to bring him his breakfast.

He hurried to the door of the cage, which his sick friend could not do, and took the ball of egg-and-potato fiercely in his beak. Then he went back to the sick bird in the corner, and gave him the whole of it without tasting it himself.

Now when Sir Philip

Sydney was being carried off the battlefield with a bad wound, he became very thirsty and begged for water.

As the cup was handed to him, a dying soldier cast upon it a look of great longing. Sydney, seeing this, would not take the cup, but said that it must be given to the soldier. "His need is greater than mine," said the dying hero.

(Sidney Lanier, adapted)

译文

鲍勃

我们养的知更鸟名叫鲍勃，但其实我们根本不该这样叫他，而应该叫他菲利普·西德尼爵士。

在乔治亚州的一个沿海小城，鲍勃从一棵大松树顶上落到我们面前。这棵树上住着许多知更鸟，这里有他们喜欢的绿叶，有海面吹来的微风，最重要的是还有充足的阳光。

那大约是三年前，鲍勃才刚刚出生几天，他躺在地上。我们不忍心将他放回树上，担心他被鹰叼走。

我们找不到他在树上的窝了，所以就亲自给他做了一个，好好地照顾他。

过了一阵子，鲍勃一想吃东西就开始大声地叫，如同被宠坏的孩子一般。有一位夫人专门照顾鲍勃，每当她把食物带来时，鲍勃就会立刻回头，张大黄色的嘴巴，然后夫人把丸子一颗接一颗地往他嘴里送，这些丸子是用蛋黄和爱尔兰土豆做的。

在与鲍勃结缘不久之后，我们把另外一只无家可归的小鸟放进鲍勃的笼子里。那时的鲍勃已经有六周大了，有一天，因为早餐迟迟未到，他饿坏了，便使出全身的力气在那大喊大叫。

最后，屋子里照顾鲍勃的夫人终于给他送来了早餐。

鲍勃匆匆忙忙地来到门边上，而另外一只小鸟却不能动弹。鲍勃十分急躁地衔起一颗鸡蛋土豆丸子，便回到角落里，把这颗丸子给了病快快的小鸟，自己一口也没吃。①

当时，人们把菲利普 · 西德尼爵士从战场上抬回来时，他伤势严重，感到很渴，就想求一口水喝。

当有人递过来一杯水时，菲利普 · 西德尼爵士注意到一位奄奄一息的士兵，他的目光满是对这杯水的渴望，于是爵士没有接过这杯水，而是执意要把这杯水让给那位士兵。“他比我更需要这杯水。”这位命悬一线的英雄说道。

（西德尼 · 拉尼尔，有删改）

作者介绍

西德尼 · 拉尼尔出生于美国乔治亚州，著有《鲍勃》一书，本文关于鲍勃的故事就选自此书。

拉尼尔也写了很多其他的故事和诗歌，其中有一些是专门为小男孩、小女孩而写的，例如《男孩心中的约瑟王》和《男孩心中的佩尔西》。

拉尼尔被称为美国作家中的加拉哈德（圣杯故事的男主角）。

① 这正是鲍勃被称作菲利普 · 西德尼爵士的原因。

The Birds and I

The springtime belongs to the birds and me. We own it.

We know when the mayflowers and the buttercups bloom. We know when the first frogs peep. We watch the opening of the woods. We are wet by the warm April rains.

We go where we will, and we are friends. Every tree and brook and blade of grass is ours; and our hearts are full of song.

There are boys who kill the birds, and girls who want to catch them and put them in cages, and there are others who steal their eggs. The birds are not friends with them; they are only servants.

Birds, like people, sing for their friends, not for their masters. I am sure that one cannot think much of the spring time and the flowers, if his heart is always set on catching something. We are happy when we are free, and so are the birds.

The birds and I get to know each other all over again every spring. They have seen strange lands in the winter, and all the brooks and the woods have been covered with snow.

So we run and romp together, and find all the nooks and corners, which we have not seen since October. The birds know the old places.

The wrens pull the sticks from the old hollow rail, and seem to be wild with joy to see the place again.

They must be the same wrens that were here last year and the year before. Strangers could not make so much fuss over an old rail.

The bluebirds and wrens look into every crack and corner for a place in which to build. The robins and the chipping-sparrows peep into every tree in the old orchard.

If the birds want to live with us, we should give them a chance. The first thing to do is to let them alone. Let them be as free from fear as you or I.

Take the hammer off the old gun, and give pussy so much to eat that she will not care to hunt for birds. Keep away the boys that steal eggs, and carry guns, and throw stones.

Plant trees and bushes about the place, and let some of them grow into tangles.

(Liberty H. Bailey, adapted)

译文

鸟儿与我

春天属于鸟儿和我，我们拥有它。

我们知道五月花和金凤花何时开花；我们知道第一只青蛙何时探出头；我们看着森林重现生机；我们被那四月的暖雨打湿。

我们想去哪里就去哪里，我们是朋友。每一棵树、每一条溪流、每一片草叶都是我们的，我们的心中满是欢歌笑语。

有杀死小鸟的男孩们，有想抓住小鸟并关进笼子里的女孩们，还有其他一些人，想偷他们的蛋。对这些人来说，鸟类并不是朋友；鸟类只是仆人。

鸟类，和人类一样，他们会为朋友歌唱，但不会为主人歌唱。我确信，如果一个人的心总是想着要获得什么，他不可能懂得欣赏春天和花朵。当自由的时候，我们才会感到快乐，鸟儿也是如此。

每年春天，我和鸟儿们都会重新相识。冬天里，他们看到了所有的小溪和树林都被大雪覆盖，也看到了远方的土地。

我们一起奔跑，一起嬉闹玩耍，寻找着那些久违的角落。自从十月份我们再也没有去过的那些老地方，鸟儿们知道怎么回去。

鹪鹩们把树枝从老旧中空的铁轨上扯走，似乎为再一次看见这个地方而欣喜若狂。

他们一定就是那群前年就在这里，去年也在这里的鹪鹩。陌生的鹪鹩不可能会对这段旧铁轨如此大惊小怪。

蓝知更鸟和鹪鹩在每一个裂缝和角落里仔细观察，寻找可以筑巢的地方。知更鸟和褐斑翅雀鹀探看这旧果园的每一棵树。

如果鸟儿们想和我们一同生活，我们应该给他们创造机会。首先要做的，就是不打扰他们，让他们像你和我一样尽可能地免受惊扰。

把旧枪支上的击铁卸下来，多给猫咪一点吃的，让她不用去抓鸟。告诉男孩们不要去偷鸟蛋，不要拿枪猎鸟，也别向鸟儿乱扔石头。

在周围多种些树和灌木，让这些树长成鸟儿们的家园。

（利伯蒂·H. 贝利，有删改）

How a Lark Learned to Sing and Fly

A baby lark tried to get out of its nest sideways and fell. It was a fall of only a foot, but a big drop for a baby.

"You can get back into the nest this way," its mother said, and showed it the way. But when the baby tried to jump, it fell.

Then the mother marked out lines on the ground, on which it was to hop. It did well, as long as the mother was there every moment to say," How well you hop!"

"Now teach me to hop up," said the little lark. It meant that it wanted to fly; and the mother tried and tried to teach it to fly. She could soar up, up, very bravely, but she could not tell how she did it.

"Wait till the sun comes out after rain," she said.

"What is sun? What is rain?" the little bird asked. "If you can not teach me to fly, teach me to sing."

"When the sun comes out after rain, then you can sing."

The rain came, and the little bird's wings were glued together. "I shall never be able to fly or to sing!" it cried.

Then it had to blink its eyes, for a light had spread over the world. The light caught every leaf and twig and blade of grass in tears, and put a smile into every tear. The baby bird's breast swelled, it did not know why; it flew from the ground, it did not know why.

"The sun has come out after the rain!" it sang."Thank you, sun! Thank you! Thank you! Oh, mother! Did you hear me? I can sing!"

Then it floated up, up, calling, "Thank you! Thank you! Thank you!" to the sun. "Oh, mother, do you see me? I am flying."

(J. M. Barrie)

译文

云雀是怎么学会歌唱与飞翔的?

小云雀试着离开鸟巢，但是它掉了下去。它也就只下落了一英尺（约三十厘米），但对一只幼鸟而言已经算很高了。

“这样你就能回鸟巢了。”小云雀的妈妈，边说边演示了一番。但当小云雀想跳起来的时候，它直接掉了下去。

于是，云雀妈妈在地上画了一条线，标注小云雀跳起来了多高。每当小云雀跳得高了一点，云雀妈妈就会说：“你跳得真棒！”

“那现在教我跳得更高吧。”小云雀说。这说明它想学飞了。于是云雀妈妈一遍又一遍地教它飞行。云雀妈妈可以飞得很漂亮，但她没法告诉小云雀自己是怎么做到的。

“还是等雨停了，太阳出来以后吧。”她说。

“太阳是什么？雨又是什么？”小云雀问道，“如果你没办法教我飞行，那就教我唱歌吧。”

“等雨停了，太阳出来以后吧，到那时你就可以唱歌了。”

下雨了，小云雀的翅膀被雨水打湿，紧紧地贴在了一起。“我既不能飞也不能唱了！”小云雀哭道。

这时，一束光照亮了整个世界，刺眼的光让小云雀不得不眨了眨眼。这束光让每一片叶子、每一个嫩枝、每一个草片上都流下了晶莹的泪珠，然后在每一滴泪水上映上了笑脸。小云雀不明白，自己的胸脯为什么会鼓了起来；也不明白自己怎么从草丛间飞了起来。

“雨停啦，太阳出来啦！”它唱道，“谢谢你太阳！谢谢你！谢谢！

哦妈妈，你听到了吗？我会唱歌啦！”

它就这样飞呀飞，边飞边对着太阳叫道：“谢谢你！谢谢！谢谢！哦妈妈，你看到了吗？我在飞翔。”

（J. M. 巴利）

Elephants and Their Babies

预习

bath /bæθ/ 洗澡

careful /ˈkerfl/ 仔细

elephant /ˈelɪfənt/ 大象

enjoy /ɪnˈdʒɔɪ/ 享受

flap /flæp/ 拍打

grand /grænd/ 宏大的

shrill /ʃrɪl/ 尖锐的

trouble /ˈtrʌbəl/ 麻烦

An elephant and her baby were alone in the great forest. The baby was only a few days old. The mother elephant had left the herd, for her little one was too small to keep up with the big elephants.

The baby elephant's eyes looked very cunning. His bit of a trunk was going up and down all the time. His ears flapped against his head, and his tail was always moving.

To his mother he was a very sweet little elephant. When she looked at him, she would often think of all the troubles and dangers that were ahead of him.

Then she would say, "As long as you are small, I shall fight for you and take care of you. When you are big, you will have to fight and run for yourself. You will have to be very careful, if you want to reach your full size."

One day she was pleased when she saw him pick up some leaves with his trunk. He put the leaves into his mouth, for the elephants use their trunks like hands. He began now to know how to get his own living. His mother loved him dearly, and stayed by his side all the time. If they met any big animal, she would give shrill cries of anger, and come close to her baby to guard him.

One night she stood close to him until daylight, for she knew that a lion was near.

As time passed away, they met other elephants with their babies. All made a large herd, and went together through the forest.

At last they came to a beautiful river. Soon after, they were all in the water swimming, throwing water with their trunks, and having great fun.

"How comfortable the water feels!" they said. "How I enjoy my bath!" So they all had a grand time. When they were swimming, the little ones rested on the backs of the mothers.

(Paul Du Chaillu, adapted)

译文

大象和她们的象宝宝

一只大象和她的小象宝宝独自在大森林中穿行，这只小象仅有几天大。大象妈妈已经离开了象群，因为她的宝宝太小了，无法跟上大象们的步伐。

小象有一双灵巧的眼睛。他那一点点短的象鼻一直在上下摆动，耳朵呼扇着脑袋，尾巴也总是动个不停。

对妈妈来说，他就是个可爱的小家伙。当她看向他时，她总会想到所有那些他即将面临的困难和危险。

于是她说："只要你还小，我都会保护你、照顾你。但等你长大，你就要为自己的生存而奋斗了。所以如果你想要长成大象，你就一定要事事小心。"

某一天，象妈妈欣慰地看到，小象已经能用象鼻捡起树叶再放到嘴里了。对大象来说，它们的象鼻就像双手一样。这说明他现在已经开始懂得要怎么独立生活了。他的妈妈深深地爱着他，并且自始至终都陪伴在他身旁。一旦碰到任何大型野兽，她就会尖声怒喊起来，靠到她的象宝宝身边，保卫着他。

某天晚上，妈妈直到天亮都寸步不离地站在象宝宝身边，因为她知道有只狮子就在附近。

过了一段时间，母子俩又遇到了其他的大象和她们的宝宝。于是所有的大象会合起来，一起穿过森林。

最终他们来到一条美丽的河流边。没一会儿，他们就一起在水里游泳，用象鼻子戏水玩耍起来。

“这水真舒服啊！”他们感慨道，“我喜欢洗澡！”就这样，他们度过了一段愉快的时光。大象们在水中游泳，小家伙们就在象妈妈们的背上休息。

（保罗·杜·沙吕，有删改）

Black Swallowtail(1)

预习

carrot /ˈkærət/ 胡萝卜

caterpillar /ˈkætərpɪlər/ 毛毛虫

hind /haɪnd/ 后部的

lemonade /ˌleməˈneɪd/ 柠檬水

scales /skeɪlz/ 鳞屑

split /splɪt/ 裂开

swallowtail /ˈswɒloʊˌteɪl/ 燕尾服

tight /taɪt/ 紧身的

whenever /wenˈevər/ 无论何时

As long as the sun shines Black Swallowtail is happy, and flies from flower to flower.

Black Swallowtail is not a bird. He is a butterfly with four broad wings, and six legs.

With his long tongue he sips nectar from flowers very much as boys and girls sip lemonade through a straw.

Swallowtail's coat looks like black velvet. It is trimmed with rows of yellow dots, and has spots of bright blue.

The real covering of his wings is made of tiny scales. These are black, yellow, and blue, and look like dust.

On the hind wings are little tails that give him his name.

As he rests on a flower, he opens and shuts his wings. He is as beautiful as a flower.

Butterflies love sunshine. When it rains they hide in the grass or bushes. They have no homes, but they know which flowers they like the best.

Black Swallowtail began his life in August last year. At that time he came out of a tiny egg.

The mother butterfly had placed the egg on a carrot leaf.

He was then not a butterfly at all, but a tiny black caterpillar, with a white spot on his back. The baby caterpillar began at once to eat. When one leaf was gone, he went to another.

Before long this greedy little fellow's coat began to feel too tight.

All at once something gave way. The coat bad split right down the back.

As this coat was now of no use, the caterpillar crept out of it, and walked away.

Strange to say he had on a new coat. It had been growing under the old one, and covered him from head to foot.

It is no wonder that the young caterpillar ate so much. He had only a few weeks in which to grow up. Winter was coming. He must be ready for a long nap.

One day he ate so much that he grew twice as long as he had been the day before, and weighed ten times as much.

Whenever his coat became too tight, it split. He would then pull himself out of it. A new coat was always ready under it.

(Mary Rogers Miller)

译文

黑色燕尾蝶（1）

只要有阳光照耀，黑色燕尾蝶便会快活起来，在花丛中飞来飞去。

黑色燕尾蝶不是鸟，而是一种蝴蝶，它有四片宽宽的蝶翼，还有六条腿。

通过长长的口器，他能从花朵中吮吸到大量花蜜，这跟孩子们用吸管喝柠檬汁的道理是一样的。

燕尾蝶的外衣看起来就像黑色的天鹅绒，上面列着几排黄色圆点，其间点缀着一些亮蓝色的斑点。

蝶翼的表面实际上由许多细小的鳞片组成，鳞片有黑色、黄色还有蓝色，看上去像粉末。

燕尾蝶两边的后翅，尾部都有一个小小的突起，他也由此而得名。

当他停在一朵花上，扑着蝶翼时，美丽的姿色与花朵不相伯仲。

蝴蝶很喜爱阳光。每当下雨，他们就躲在草丛或灌木丛中。他们没有家，但十分清楚哪种花是自己心中的最爱。

在前一年的八月份，黑色燕尾蝶的生命旅程就开始了。这时，他还是一颗小小的虫卵。

他的妈妈会把卵产到胡萝卜的叶子上。

然后，他变成了一条黑色的小毛毛虫，背上长着白色的斑点，没有一点蝴蝶的样子。年幼的毛毛虫马上就开始吃起了叶子。一片吃完，他就爬到另外一片上面去。

要不了多久，这个贪吃的小家伙就会感到外衣很紧了。

突然，情况就失去了控制。他的外衣在背上裂了一条大缝。

旧外衣已经失去作用，毛毛虫从里面爬了出来，离开了。

要是说他穿着新衣服，是有点奇怪的。新外衣其实是从旧外衣底下长出来的，把他从头到脚地包了起来。

小毛毛虫的生长期只有短短的几周，也难怪他的食量那么大。冬天一来，他就要准备进入漫长的休眠期了。

他吃得特别多，在一天之内，身子就能比前一天长长一倍，体重则能达到前一天的十倍之多。

只要他的外衣变得很紧，就会随时裂开。他从旧衣服里面爬出来的时候，新的外衣则已经在旧衣服底下准备好了。

（玛丽 · 罗杰斯 · 米勒）

Black Swallowtail(2)

When October came, the Swallowtail caterpillar was nearly two inches long. The coat that he now wore was bright green with black stripes and rows of yellow dots. The caterpillar was restless. He no longer held fast to a leaf, but started out to see the world.

Pretty soon he walked along the garden fence and crept under a board. Then he stood still, and began to wag his head from side to side. He was spinning.

First he made a silk rope, and fastened both ends to the board to form a loop. He then spun a tiny rug to rest his feet upon.

When these were done, he put his head through the loop of silk, and clung fast to the little rug.

The next day he cast aside his bright green coat. He was not a caterpillar any longer. He was a chrysalis, and nearly the color of the fence.

A woodpecker looking for food in the winter might walk

right by and never see the dull, brown chrysalis.

All winter Black Swallowtails chrysalis hung there on the board. In May his covering was again too small for him.

The chrysalis moved. Pretty soon the winter coat split. The sleeper crept out.

At first he was very weak. He stretched himself, and began to grow stronger. His wings, too, began to spread.

Swallowtail had been an egg, a caterpillar, and a chrysalis. At last he was a full grown butterfly.

(Mary Rogers Miller)

译文

黑色燕尾蝶（2）

当十月来临，燕尾蝶毛毛虫就差不多有两英寸（约五厘米）长了。他现在的外衣是明亮的绿色，夹杂着黑色条纹和几排黄色的圆点。毛毛虫不安分起来，开始张望外面的世界，不再紧抓着一片树叶不放了。

过了不久，他沿着花园的篱笆爬到一块木板底下，停了下来。他把脑袋从这儿摆到那儿，开始做起了纺织活。

首先，他织了一股丝绳，两端固定在木板上，做成一个圈。然后，他又开始织起一张小毯子，好让他的脚能放在上面。

做完这些事以后，他把脑袋穿过用丝绳做好的圈子，紧紧地贴在那块小毯子上。

第二天，他把他的绿外衣丢到一边去了。他不再是一只毛毛虫了，是一只蝶蛹。蛹的颜色非常接近篱笆的颜色。

这样，冬天啄木鸟在觅食的时候，也许永远注意不到这个不起眼的棕色蝶蛹，就能忽视这个蝶蛹的存在。

一整个冬天，黑色燕尾蝶的蝶蛹都挂在板子上。到了五月，外面包着的蛹对他来说已经太小了。

蛹抖动着。不久后，这层冬衣裂开了，在里面睡觉的小家伙爬了出来。

一开始，他非常虚弱。后来，他伸展着身体，慢慢地变得强壮起来。他的翅膀，也开始伸展开来。

燕尾蝶经历了卵、毛虫和蝶蛹的形态，最终变成了一只发育成熟的蝴蝶。

（玛丽·罗杰斯·米勒）

Sponges

Ruth and Mark were at Key West in Florida with their father and mother. One day the children rowed out to see the sponging fleet. These are the boats that gather sponges.

An old sponger kindly told the children about the sponges. "Did you ever hear of a water glass?" he asked.

"No," said Ruth," I never did."

"Here is one. Perhaps you would like to look at it." And he showed them what looked like a wooden bucket with a glass bottom. "Just hold it a little way down in the water, and see what you can see."

Ruth took the bucket and looked."Oh, I can see the bottom of the sea just as clearly as looking through a window."

"To be sure," said the old sponger, "that is the way that we see the sponges lying on the bottom. Then we take these long rakes and draw the sponges to the top.

"When the sponges first come up, they are black. We throw them all into a pond of clear water. After they have stayed there for sometime, we stir them up and beat them. That is to make them clean.

"Then the sponges have to be washed and dried and trimmed. After that they are ready to send to market."

Before Ruth and Mark went home, they saw a funny sight. They saw little black boys diving deep into the water to bring up sponges that the rakes had missed.

(Kirk Munroe, adapted)

译文

海绵

露丝和马克还有他们的爸爸妈妈都住在佛罗里达的基韦斯特。一天，露丝和马克跑出去看海绵船队。海绵船队就是捕捞海绵的船队。

一位和蔼的老海绵工为这两个孩子讲述了海绵的故事。“你们听说过一种叫作水玻璃的东西吗？”他问。

“没有，”露丝说，“我从来没有听说过。”

“我这儿就有一个。或许你们想要看看。”说着，老海绵工拿出了一个东西给他们看，这个东西像一个装有玻璃底座的木桶。“你们拿着它，把它在水里稍微浸一下，然后看看你们能看到什么。”

露丝拿着那个桶观察起来。“哇，透过这个底座看海就像隔着玻璃一样清楚。”

“那当然，”老海绵工说，“我们看到的一些附着在海底的海绵。接下来我们要用长耙将这些海绵捞上来。

“这些海绵刚刚出水时是黑色的。我们要把它们全部扔进干净的水池里。放上一段时间后，我们搅拌一下这些海绵，然后敲打。这样海绵就会变得干干净净了。

“接下来，这些海绵经过清洁、烘干以及切割之后，就可以送到市场上去出售了。”

在露丝和马克回家之前，他们看到了一幕有趣的场景：有几个黑人小男孩潜到深深的海水中，去采集一些长耙漏下的海绵。

（柯克 · 门罗，有删改）

Chapter 3

Miscellaneous Poems | 杂诗

September

预习

bare /ber/ 赤裸的
bending /ˈbendɪŋ/ 弯曲的
chill /tʃɪl/ 使变冷
golden-rod /ˈgəʊldənrˈɒd/ 一枝黄花
noon /nuːn/ 正午

The golden-rod is yellow;
The corn is turning brown;
The trees in apple orchards
With fruit are bending down.

(Helen Hunt Jackson, adapted)

译文

九月

一枝金花黄又黄，
玉米成熟变了装，
苹果园里还有树，
果子成熟压弯梁。

（亨利 · D. 索罗，有删改）

练习

秋天是一年中万物飘零的季节，属于秋天的月份有九月、十月和十一月。

(1)月份的首字母有何特点?

(2)诗每一行的首字母有何特点?

抄写下列陈述句。

Warm September brings the fruit;
Sportsmen then begin to shoot.

Fresh October brings the pheasant;
Then to gather nuts is pleasant.

Dull November brings the blast;
Then the leaves fall thick and fast.

(Sara Coleridge)

October

Warm September brings the fruit;
Sportsmen then begin to shoot.
Fresh October brings the pheasant;
Then to gather nuts is pleasant.
Dull November brings the blast;
Then the leaves fall thick and fast.

(Sara Coleridge)

译文

十月

暖秋九月，瓜果成熟，
猎人上山忙打猎。
金色十月，野鸡出现，
去捡坚果兴高采烈。
寂寞十一月，大风不歇，
飞过阵阵旋转的树叶。

（萨拉·科尔里奇）

November

November woods are bare and still;
November days are clear and bright;
Each noon burns up the morning's chill;
The morning's snow is gone by night.
Trees bare and brown,
Dry leaves everywhere,
Dancing up and down,
Flying through the air.
Red-cheeked apples roasted,
Popcorn almost done,
Toes and chestnuts toasted,
That's November fun.

(Helen Hunt Jackson)

译文

十一月

十一月的树林静谧荒芜，
十一月的天空明亮澄澈；
清晨的寒意总被正午驱逐；
早晨的雪花下不到夜幕。
树丛干枯荒芜，
枯叶藏身在每一处，
忽上忽下，
漫天飞舞。
红彤彤的苹果上了烤炉，
爆米花就要烤熟，
边暖着脚趾边烤栗子，
这是十一月的乐处。

（海伦·亨特·杰克逊）

练习

1. 抄写并完成：

My full name is ___________.
My father's name is ___________.
My mother's name is ___________.
My teacher's name is ___________.

2. 这些名字的各个部分分别是什么形式的字母开头？

The Knights and the Child

Galloping fast and galloping free,
Who comes a-riding so swift to me?

"Over the world we ride, to find
The child that is loving and good and kind."

This is the child so dear!
Brave knights, you see him here!

"O child, be always good and gay.
Now gallop and gallop and gallop away."

(Emily Huntingdon Miller)

译文

骑士与孩童

是谁，跑得飞快，跑得欢快，
正向我奔来？

“我们满世界骑行，到处寻找，
善良纯朴的可爱孩子。”

看这个小孩，
勇敢的骑士，你瞧他多么讨人喜爱！

“孩子你要永远喜笑颜开，不见阴霾，
现在我要跑啊，跑啊，跑远啦。”

（艾米丽 · 亨廷顿 · 米勒）

The Chestnut Burr

The wind cried aloud to the chestnut burr,
"Open, come open to me!"
And he blew with his might
Till the burr shook with fright,
But never a bit opened she.

Then the sun smiled down on the little green burr,
"Please open," he coaxed, "to me!"
And he shone so warm,
That the burr in alarm
Hid under the leaves of the tree.

Jack Frost came hurrying down the hill.
"Ho, ho, ha, ha!" laughed he.
And the burr laughed back,
Till her brown sides cracked;
Then out fell the chestnuts three.

(Christine H. Hamilton)

译文

板栗毛刺

狂风对着板栗毛刺大声叫：
“快迎接我，打开你的怀抱。”
狂风吹呀吹，大声呼号，
吓得毛刺瑟瑟发抖，
但她一点儿缝都没开。

太阳来了，对着青色的小毛刺微笑，
“请打开吧，”他哄骗道，“为我打开你的衣壳。”
接着他的光芒更加闪耀，
那刺眼的光却让毛刺警觉，
于是悄悄藏进树叶间。

严寒匆匆来到山脚，
对着毛刺“哈哈”大笑。
逗得毛刺轻笑，
直到笑开了棕色的衣壳；
三颗栗子跳出了毛刺的怀抱。

（克里斯汀·H. 汉密尔顿）

练习

分别写出风、太阳和严寒对毛刺说的话。

Good-Night

预习

beginning /bɪˈɡɪnɪŋ/ 开始

light /laɪt/ 光

watch /wɒtʃ/ 看

Good-night, pretty Sun, good-night;
I have watched your purple and golden light.
While you are sinking away,
And some one has just been telling me,
You're making, over the shining sea,
Another beautiful day:
That just at the time I am going to sleep,
The children there are taking a peep,
At your face-beginning to say,
"Good-morning!" just when I say,
"Good-night!"
Now, beautiful Sun, if they've told me right,
I wish you would say good-morning for me,
To all the little ones over the sea.

(Sydney Dayre)

译文

晚安

晚安，美丽的太阳，晚安；
我看到了你紫金色的光芒，
而你却快要消失踪影。
曾有人对我说过，
你会在清辉闪烁的海洋的另一头，
创造另一个美丽的白昼：
那时，我已爬上了我的小床，
而另一边的孩子们却在偷看你的脸，
在我对你说“晚安”时，
那里的孩子正要轻道
“早安”！
如果他们说的是真的，那么美丽的太阳，
那么我希望你能把我的早安
带给海那头的孩子们。

（悉尼·戴尔）

The New Moon

Dear mother, how pretty
The moon looks to-night;
She was never so pretty before;
Her two little horns
Are so sharp and so bright,
Hope she'll not grow any more.

If I were up there,
With you and my friends,
I'd rock in it nicely, you'd see;
I'd sit in the middle
And hold by both ends.
Oh, what a bright cradle. It would be!

And there we would rock
In the beautiful skied,
And through the bright clouds we would roam;
We would see the sun set,
And see the sun rise,
And on the next rainbow come home.

(Eliza Lee Follen)

译文

新月

亲爱的妈妈，你瞧
今夜的月亮多么迷人；
她从未如此美丽；
瞧她的月梢，
尖尖的月梢多么明亮，
真希望她永远都是月牙不要长大。

如果我能和你还有我的朋友，
一同升到那天空，
你会看到，我坐上月亮船，
双手抓住小船的两端，
温柔地将她摇动。
哦！那会是多么明亮的摇篮啊！

而我们会摇着月亮船，
在这夜空翱翔，
我们会穿过层层云朵，自在徜徉；
我们还会看见日落，
看到日出，
然后在下一次的彩虹升空时回家。

（伊莱扎・李・福林）

The Land of Story Books

At evening when the lamp is lit,
Around the fire my parents sit;
They sit at home and talk and sing,
And do not play at anything.

Now, with my little gun, I crawl
All in the dark along the wall,
And follow round the forest track
Away behind the sofa back.
There in the night, where none can spy,
All in my hunter's camp I lie,
And play at books that I have read,
Till it is time to go to bed.

So, when my nurse comes in for me,
Home I return across the sea,
And go to bed with backward looks
At my dear land of Story Books.

(Robert Louis Stevenson)

译文

故事书的乐园

夜幕降临，灯光朗朗，
爸爸妈妈坐在炉火旁；
他们在家又说又唱，
再不管其他事情。

而我正扛着小枪，
在黑夜中匍匐沿着墙，
似是穿行于林间小巷，
只是在沙发后面躲藏。
夜晚已经来临，没有人偷瞄，
只有我躺在帐篷笑闹，
随意翻看读过的书，
直到到点上床睡觉。

于是，当保姆向我走来，
我穿过大海回到了家，
爬上床却还在留恋徘徊，
徘徊在我最亲爱的故事乐园。

（罗伯特·路易斯·斯蒂文森）

练习

写出这首小诗的所有韵脚。

The Water Mill(1)

预习

between /bɪˈtwiːn/ 在……之间

blind /blaɪnd/ 盲的

flap /flæp/ 拍打

grind /graɪnd/ 磨

grist /grɪst/ 磨粉的谷物；有利的事

merrily /ˈmerəli/ 欢乐的

mill /mɪl/ 磨坊

oxen /ˈɒksn/ 牛

pack /pæk/ 一群

pour /pɔːr/ 倾倒

yoke /joʊk/ 轭

"Any grist for the mill?"
How merrily it goes!
Flap, flap, flap, flap,
While the water flows.
Round-about and round-about,
The heavy mill-stones grind,

And the dust flies all about the mill,
And makes the miller blind.

"Any grist for the mill?"
The busy farmer packs
His wagon with a heavy load
Of very heavy sacks.
Then drives his yoke of oxen
To mill, at early morn,
And between the greedy mill-stones
Is poured the golden corn.

"Any grist for the mill?"
The backers come and go;
They bring their open sacks to fill,
And leave them down below.
The dusty miller and his men
Fill all the sacks they bring,
And while they go about their work
Right merrily they sing.

译文

水车（1）

“有要磨的粮食吗？”
瞧它的转动是多么欢快啊！
只要水在流动，
它就转啊转啊转不停。
转啊转啊转，
沉沉的石磨咯吱响，
尘土到处飞扬，
遮住了水车的脸庞。

“有要磨的粮食吗？”
忙碌的农民开始收拾东西
装满了大大的麻袋，
塞进了他的车子，
然后架上了牛车，
大清早就往磨坊赶去。
不一会儿，贪吃的石磨间
盛满了金黄的玉米。

“有要磨的粮食吗？”
人们来了又走，走了又来；

他们带来了敞口的麻袋，
丢在了石磨的脚边。
而满身灰尘的石磨和他的主人，
努力填满那些袋子
每当他们开始工作，
还会欢乐地歌唱。

The Water Mill(2)

Living close beside the mill,
The miller's girls and boys
Always play at make-believe,
Because they have no toys.

"Any grist for our mill?"
The older brothers shout,
While all the little maidens
Go dancing round-about.

"Any grist for the mill?"
How quickly it goes around!
Flap, flap, flap, flap,
What a merry sound!
The children laugh right gayly,
As with clacking tongue it sings
Of Johnny-cake for breakfast.
And other pleasant things.

"Any grist for the mill?"
But see! It will not go;
The river, too, is standing still,
The ground is white with snow.

And when the frosty season comes,
And freezes up the streams,
The miller only hears the mill,
And grinds the corn in dreams.

The miller's little boys and girls
Are glad to see the snow.
"Good father, play with us to-day;
You cannot work, you know.
We will be the mill-stones,
And you shall be the wheel;
We'll toss the white snow all about,
And it shall be the meal."

Oh, heartily the miller's wife
Laughs at the kitchen door.
She never saw the miller work
So merrily before:
"Bravely done, my little lads,
Start up the lazy wheel,
For money comes but slowly in
When snow-flakes are the meal."

译文

水车（2）

在磨坊旁，
住着磨坊主的孩子们，
孩子们总是玩幻想游戏，
因为他们并没有玩具。

“有要磨的粮食吗？”
哥哥大声喊道，
而小姑娘们
却跑去跳舞玩耍。

“有要磨的粮食吗？”
看它转得那样飞快！
啪啪，啪啪，啪啪，
多么美妙的声音！
孩子们欢快的笑声，
伴着石磨咔哒咔哒的歌声，
他在为美味的早餐歌唱，
为所有美好的事物歌唱。

“有要磨的粮食吗？”

但是快看啊！他不走了；
河水也静止不流了，
地上已铺满了洁白的雪花。
严寒就要来了，
小溪也要结冰了，
而磨坊主呀，只能在梦里听到石磨的转动声，
在梦里磨玉米。

磨坊主可爱的孩子们，
看到下雪可是乐坏了。
“好爸爸好爸爸，今天就陪我们玩吧；
反正你也知道今天没法工作了；
我们当磨石，
你来扮轮子；
然后让这漫天的雪花，
做我们要碾碎的玉米。”

哦，磨坊主的妻子站在厨房门口，
看到这一幕由衷地笑了。
她从没见过磨坊主这样快乐，
这样快乐地干活：
“勇敢去做，我的孩子，
快快转动那懒惰的轮子，
因为让雪花做谷物，
你们就没法快快赚钱了。”

The Child and the Bird

预习

bloom /bluːm/ 繁茂

forget /fərˈget/ 忘记

gloom /gluːm/ 使变得阴沉

stir /stɜːr/ 搅动

storm /stɔːrm/ 风暴

"Oh, where are you going, my dear little bird?
And why do you hurry away?
Not a leaf on the pretty red maple has stirred,
In the sweet golden sunshine to-day."

"I know, little maiden, the sunshine is bright,
And the leaves are asleep on the tree,
But three times the dream of cold winter's night
Has come to my children and me."

"So, good-by to you, darling, for off we must go,
To the land where the oranges bloom,
For we birdies would freeze in the storms and the snow,

And forget how to sing in the gloom."

"Will you ever come back to your own little nest?"
"Ah, yes, when the blossoms are here,
We'll return to the orchard we all love the best,
And then we will sing to you, dear."

(Margaret E. Sangster)

译文

孩子与鸟

"哦，我亲爱的小鸟，你要飞往哪里去？
那美丽的枫叶还未落下，
金色的阳光依然笼罩，
而你为什么要匆匆离开呢？"

"我知道，小姑娘，阳光依然灿烂，
叶子也还在树枝上静静安睡，
但是那寒冷的冬夜
已经三次潜入我和孩子们的睡梦里。"

"那么，再见了我亲爱的你，我们很快就要离去。
我们要飞去的地方，橘树还欣欣向荣，
因为寒冷的暴风雪会让我们冻僵，
并忘记怎么歌唱。"

"那你还会回来吗？回到你的小巢？"
"当然会，等花儿再次开放，
我们就会回到我们最爱的果园，
还会继续为你歌唱。"

（玛格丽特·伊丽莎白·桑斯特）

A Boy's Song

Where the pools are bright and deep,
Where the gray trout lies asleep,
Up the river and over the lea——
That's the way for Billy and me.

Where the blackbird sings the latest,
Where the hawthorn blooms the sweetest,
Where the nestlings chirp and flee——
That's the way for Billy and me.

Where the mowers mow the cleanest,
Where the hay lies thick and greenest;
There to trace the homeward bee——
That's the way for Billy and me.

Where the hazel bank is steepest,
Where the shadow fall the deepest,
Where the clustering nuts fall free——
That's the way for Billy and me.

(James Hogg)

译文

男孩之歌

哪里的池塘深又清，
哪里有灰鳟鱼静静入睡，
在那河流和草地上，
是我和比利玩耍的地方。

哪里的画眉在歌唱，
哪里的山楂最美地绽放，
哪里的小鸟叽叽喳喳地逃窜，
哪里就是我和比利探索的地方。

哪里的割草机割草最棒，
哪里的草垛又厚又绿最适合躺；
这里是蜜蜂回家的地方，
更是我和比利的天堂。

哪里的榛木林最陡峭，
哪里的树影最长最高，
哪里的坚果落不停，
哪里就是我和比利探寻的方向。

（詹姆斯·霍格）

Thanksgiving Day

Over the river and through the wood,
To grandfather's house we go;
The horse knows the way
To carry the sleigh
Through the white and drifted snow.

Over the river and through the wood,
Trot fast, my dapple-gray!
Spring over the ground,
Like a hunting hound!
For this is Thanksgiving Day.

Over the river and through the wood.
And straight through the barn-yard gate,
We seem to go
Extremely slow——
It is so hard to wait!

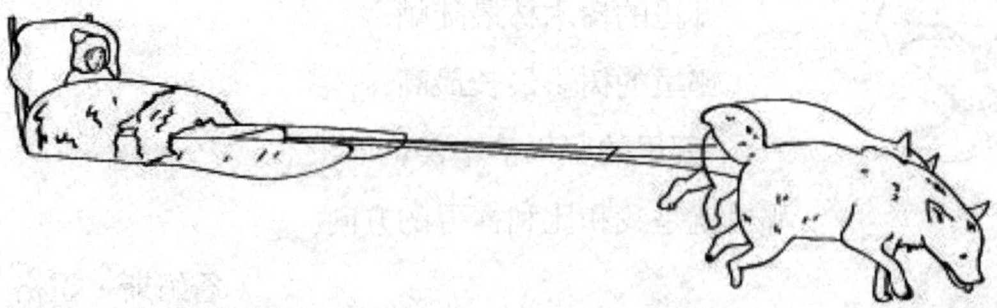

Over the river and through the wood——
Now grandmother's cap I spy!
Hurrah for the fun!
Is the pudding done?
Hurrah for the pumpkin pie!

(Lydia Maria Child)

译文

感恩节

踏过河流，穿越树林，
我们去祖父家；
识路的马儿啊，
正拉着雪橇
带着我们穿过飞舞的白雪。

踏过河流，穿越树林，
我可爱的马儿快快跑！
快点跳过这土地，
像那飞奔的猎犬！
只因这是感恩节。

踏过河流，穿越树林
径直穿过谷仓院子的大门，
我们的速度
还是太过缓慢——
漫长的等待太难捱！

踏过河流，穿越树林——
祖母的家终于映入了眼帘！

冲啊！为了快乐快点冲！

祖母的布丁做好了吗？

冲啊！为了南瓜派快点冲！

（莉迪亚·玛丽亚·蔡尔德）

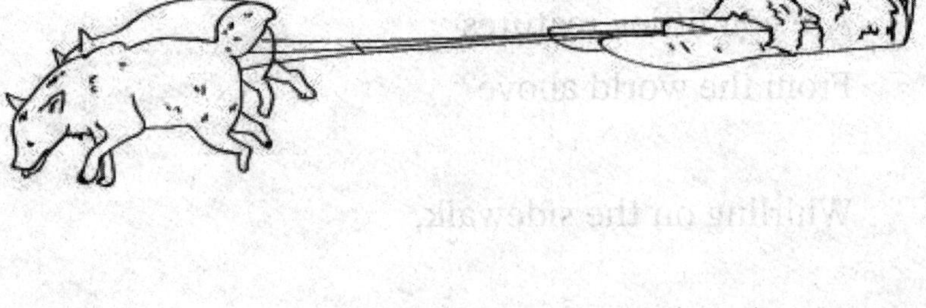

Snowflakes

预习

angel /ˈendʒəl/ 天使

creature /ˈkriːtʃəz/ 造物

cunning /ˈkʌnɪŋ/ 狡猾的

loading /ˈloʊdɪŋ/ 降落

powdering /ˈpaʊdərɪŋ/ 粉末

spotless /ˈspɑːtləs/ 洁白无瑕

whirling /ˈwɜːlɪŋ/ 旋转

Tiny little snowflakes,
In the air so high,
Are you little angels,
Floating in the sky?

Robed so white and spotless,
Flying like a dove,
Are you little creatures
From the world above?

Whirling on the sidewalk,

Dancing in the street,
Kissing all the faces
Of the children sweet.

Loading all the housetops,
Powdering all the trees——
Cunning little snowflakes,
Little busy bees!

(Lucy Larcom)

译文

雪花

可爱的小雪花，
在高高的天空玩耍，
你是小天使吗？我的小雪花，
是游走在天空的天使吧？

身穿白衣洁白无瑕，
像那白鸽漫天飞舞，
你是小精灵吗？我的小雪花，
是来自另一个世界的精灵吧？

人行道旁回旋，
街道上飞舞，
轻轻吻落在
每一个孩子甜甜的脸庞。

落在每一个屋顶，
飘洒在所有树上——
瞧这可爱的小雪花，
简直是忙碌的小蜜蜂！

（露西 · 拉科姆）

练习

写出这首诗里所有以ing结尾的单词。

The Owl

When cats run home and light is come,
And dew is cold upon the ground,
And the far-off stream is dumb,
And the whirring sail goes round,
And the whirring sail goes round;
Alone and warming his five wits,
The white owl in the belfry sits.

(Lord Alfred Tennyson)

译文

猫头鹰

当小猫回到房屋，灯儿点亮，
露水落在冰凉的草地上，
远方的溪流不再流淌，
船儿呼啸着四处远航，
船儿呼啸着四处远航；
白色的猫头鹰静坐钟楼上，
形影相吊，无所不晓。

（阿尔弗雷德·丁尼生）

The Snow-Bird's Song

预习

already /ɔːlˈredi/ 已经
clothe /kloʊð/ 穿上
parlor /ˈpɑːlə/ 客厅
stockings /sˈtɒkɪŋz/ 长袜
though /ðoʊ/ 尽管
tune /tuːn/ 曲子

The ground was all covered with snow one day,
And two little sisters were busy at play,
When a snow-bird was sitting close by, on a tree
And merrily singing his chick-a-dee-dee,
Chick-a-dee-dee, chick-a-dee-dee.

He had not been singing that tune very long
Ere Emily heard him, so loud was his song.
"Oh, sister, look out of the window!" said she,
"Here's a dear little bird, singing chick-a-dee-dee,
Chick-a-dee-dee, chick-a-dee-dee,
Here's a dear little bird, singing chick-a-dee-dee."

"Oh, mother, do get him some stockings and shoes,
And a nice little coat, and a hat if he choose;
I wish he'd come into the parlor and see
How warm we would make him, poor chick-a-dee-dee!
Chick-a-dee-dee, chick-a-dee-dee,
How warm we would make him, poor chick-a-dee-dee!"

"There is One, my dear child, though I cannot tell who,
Has clothed me already, and warm enough, too.
Good-morning! ——oh, who are so happy as we?"
And away he went, singing his chick-a-dee-dee;
Chick-a-dee-dee, chick-a-dee-dee;
And away he went, singing his chick-a-dee-dee.

(F. G. Woodworth)

译文

雪鸟之歌

一天，大雪淹没了大地，
一对小姐妹正在玩闹，
一只雪鸟停在了附近的一棵树上，
用甜美的嗓音欢快歌唱，
嘁呵——啊——嘀嘀。

他已很久没有唱起这样的曲调，
艾米丽听到了他的高唱。
“哦，姐姐，快看窗户外面！”她说，
“那儿有一只可爱的小鸟，正在‘嘁呵——啊——嘀嘀’地歌唱，
嘁呵——啊——嘀嘀，
那儿有一只可爱的小鸟，正在‘嘁呵——啊——嘀嘀’地歌唱。”

“哦，妈妈，快给他拿些厚袜和冬靴，
一件漂亮的小外套，他需要的话再加顶帽子；
真希望他能来我们的家看看，
他该有多暖和，可怜的小鸟！
只是在唱‘嘁呵——啊——嘀嘀’，
他该有多暖和，可怜的小鸟！”

“这儿已经有衣服了，我亲爱的孩子，

虽然我也不知道是谁给我穿上了这温暖的衣裳。

真是个美妙的早晨！——是谁让我们这样快乐啊？”

说完他就飞走了，依旧唱着“嘁呵——啊——嘀嘀”的歌谣；

嘁呵——啊——嘀嘀；

说完他就飞走了，依旧唱着“嘁呵——啊——嘀嘀”的歌谣。

（F. G. 伍德沃斯）

The Arrow and the Song

I shot an arrow into the air,
It fell to earth, I know not where;
For, so swiftly it flew, the sight
Could not follow it in its flight.
I breathed a song into the air,
It fell to earth, I know not where;
For who has sight so keen and strong,
That it can follow the flight of song?

(Henry Wadsworth Longfellow)

译文

箭与歌

我向天空射出一支箭，
它却在不知名的角落，无影无踪；
它飞得那样急、那样快，
视线无法跟上它的脚步。
我向天空轻唱一首歌，
它却在不知名的角落，无影无踪；
谁的眼力这样强，
能追上歌声的飞扬？

（亨利·沃兹沃斯·朗费罗）

背景知识

下面这封信写于朗费罗七岁那年：

Portland, January, 1814.

Dear Papa,

Ann wants a Bible like little Betsey's. Will you please buy her one if you can find any in Boston?

I have been to school all the week and got only seven

marks. I shall have a billet on Monday.

I wish you to buy me a drum.

H.W.L.

译文：

亲爱的爸爸：

安想要一辆像贝奇骑的自行车。如果你在波士顿看到那种样式的车子，能麻烦你买一辆给她吗？

整个一周我都去上学了，却只拿了七分。周一我就可以住宿了。

好希望你能给我买一架鼓。

亨利 · 沃兹沃斯 · 朗费罗

写于波特兰，1814 年1 月

作者介绍

亨利 · 沃兹沃斯 · 朗费罗被誉为“儿童诗人”，他出生于美国波特兰，诗集《我逝去的青春》里有一首《美丽的乡村》有涉及他最早生活的家。他的晚年在剑桥度过。

朗费罗写过一些散文，但他的大部分时间还是献给了诗歌。他的代表作有《楼梯上的旧钟》《乡村铁匠》《米尼辛克的墓地》《待赎畜栏中的飞马》《基林沃斯的鸟》《建筑工人》《诺尔曼男爵》《伊凡吉林》《海华沙之歌》《大天使圣德芬》《迈尔斯 · 斯坦迪什的求婚》。

A Christmas Song

预习

brood /bruːd/ 一窝

Christmas /ˈkrɪsməs/ 圣诞节

courage /ˈkɜːrɪdʒ/ 勇气

dread /dred/ 害怕

hatred /ˈheɪtrɪd/ 憎恨

patient /ˈpeɪʃnt/ 耐心

peace /piːs/ 和平

peak /piːk/ 顶峰

pity /ˈpɪti/ 怜悯

solemn /ˈsɑːləm/ 庄严的

sorrow /ˈsɑːroʊ/ 悲伤

Everywhere, everywhere, Christmas to-night!
Christmas in lands of fir tree and pine;
Christmas in lands of palm tree and vine;
Christmas where snow peaks stand solemn and white;
Christmas where cornfields lie sunny and bright:
Everywhere, everywhere, Christmas to-night!

Christmas where children are hopeful and gay;
Christmas where old men are patient and gray;
Christmas where peace, like a dove in its flight,
Broods over brave men in the thick of the fight;
Everywhere, everywhere, Christmas to-night!

Then let every heart keep its Christmas within,
Christ's pity for sorrow, Christ's hatred for sin,
Christ's care for the weakest, Christ's courage for right,
Christ's dread of the darkness, Christ's love of the light,
Everywhere, everywhere, Christmas to-night!

(Phillips Brooks)

译文

圣诞歌

圣诞到，圣诞到，圣诞处处闹！
圣诞穿过枞树林与松树林间；
圣诞亲吻着棕榈树与藤蔓的笑颜；
圣诞在晶莹素雅的雪花中；
圣诞还在谷仓温暖明媚的阳光里；
圣诞到，圣诞到，圣诞处处闹！

圣诞在孩子们满是希望与喜悦的笑声里；
圣诞在老人灰白的发丝里；
圣诞在和平鸽飞过的地方，
在孩子们或勇士们酣战的方向；
圣诞到，圣诞到，圣诞处处闹！

来吧，来让每一颗心都沉浸在圣诞里，
同情不幸，谴责罪恶，
关爱弱者，鼓励正义，
畏惧黑暗，热爱光明，
圣诞到，圣诞到，圣诞处处闹！

（菲利普·布鲁克）

The Bright Side

The sun is gone down,
And the moon's in the sky;
But the sun will come up,
And the moon be laid by.
The flower is asleep,
But it is not dead;
When the morning shines,
It will lift its head.

(Eofge Macdonald)

译文

光明的一边

太阳已落入山间，
月亮出现在天边；
太阳会再度露面，
月亮也会消失不见。
花朵悄悄入睡，
但它还未衰颓；
当晨光熠熠生辉，
它会再度抬起头颅。

（乔治·麦克唐纳）

练习

抄写这首诗，并写出诗中的韵脚。

Talking in Their Sleep

"You think I am dead,"
The apple tree said.
"Because I have never a leaf to show;
Because I stoop,
And my branches droop,
And the dull gray mosses over me grow.
But I am alive in trunk and root;
The buds of next May
I fold away——
But I pity the withered grass at my root."

"You think I am dead,"
The quick grass said.
"Because I have parted with stem and blade;
But under the ground
I am safe and sound,
With the snow's thick blanket over me laid.
I'm all alive, and ready to shoot,
Should the spring of the year
Come dancing here——
But I pity the flower without branch or root."

"You think I am dead,"

A soft voice said.
"Because not a branch or a root I own.
I never have died,
But close I hide
In the plumy seed that the wind has sown.
Patient I wait through the long winter hours.
You will see me again,——
I shall laugh at you then,
Out of the eyes of a hundred flowers."

(Edith M. Thomas)

译文

梦呓

“你觉得我要死了，”
苹果树说，
“因为我的叶子都掉光了；
因为我看着像是停止了生长，
我的树枝干枯下垂
我的身上长满了灰暗的苔藓。
但我的树干和根还活着；
等到了明年五月，
我又会长出新芽——
只是，我为根上的枯草感到惋惜。”

“你觉得我要死了，”
茅草说，
“因为我的茎叶已经凋落；
但在地下的我啊，
还安全完好，
雪花给我铺就了薄薄的毯子，
我还活着，随时准备着发芽，
等春天，跳着舞来到这里，
我就能破土而出——

但我还是为那些没有根枝的花朵感到惋惜。”

“你觉得我要死了，”
一个轻柔的声音说道，
“因为我既没有枝干也没有根，
我从来不会死，
我只是藏了起来，
藏在了微风播撒的种子里。
我耐心地熬过漫长的冬天。
你将再次看到我——
看到我在百花丛中，
对你笑。”

（伊迪斯·玛蒂尔达·托马斯）

A Lullaby

Rains beat! Winds blow!
Safe the nest in the elm tree.
Days come! Nights go!
Birds at rest in the elm tree.
To-and-fro, to-and-fro,
Safe are we from every foe——
Cats come! Cats go!
Lullaby in the elm tree.

(Mabel Osgood Wright)

译文

摇篮曲

雨儿落！风儿吹！
榆树中的巢里安心睡。
天亮了！夜走了！
榆树丛里鸟儿在休息。
来来去去，去去来来，
远离天敌的伤害——
猫来了！又走了！
榆树中响起摇篮曲。

（梅布尔·奥斯古德·赖特）

The Poet and His Boat

预习

balloon /bəˈluːn/ 气球

beneath /bɪˈniːθ/ 在下方

breathless /ˈbreθləs/ 呼吸困难的

crescent /ˈkresnt/ 新月

ether /ˈiːθər/ 天空

perchance /pərˈtʃæns/ 或许

thousand /ˈθaʊznd/ 千

There's something in a flying horse,
There's something in a huge balloon;
But through the clouds I'll never float
Until I have a little boat,
For shape just like the crescent moon.
And now I have a little boat,
In shape a very crescent moon:
Fast through the clouds my boat can sail;
But, if perchance your faith should fail,
Look up, and you shall see me soon.
Up goes my boat among the stars

Through many a breathless field of light,
Through many a long blue field of either,
Leaving ten thousand stars beneath her:
Up goes my little boat so bright!

(William Wordsworth)

译文

诗人与舟

飞马里一定有什么东西，
巨型气球里一定有什么东西；
但我绝不会穿过云层
除非我得到一叶小舟，
就像新月的模样。
现在我有了一叶小舟，
就像一枚完美的新月：
我的小舟飞速穿过云层；
如果你的信念偶尔动摇，
抬头望，你会看见我。
我的小舟飞升至群星之间
穿过令人窒息的光域，
穿过蓝色的苍穹，
在她的怀抱下留下一万颗星星：
我的小舟一直闪亮地飞升上去！

（威廉·华兹华斯）

The Flower

Once in a golden hour
I cast to earth a seed.
Up there came a flower,
The people said a weed.

Then it grew so tall
It wore a crown of light,
But thieves from over the wall,
Stole the seed by night.
Sowed it far and wide
By every town and tower,
Till all the people cried,
"Splendid is the flower."

(Lord Alfred Tennyson)

译文

花

曾经在一个美妙的时刻，
我在地里埋下了一颗种子。
很快那里就长出了一株花，
而人们却说那只是棵杂草。

很快它就长大了
戴上了光之冠，
但小偷从墙的那侧翻过来，
趁着黑夜偷走了种子。
在每一座小镇和塔边，
都撒下了种子，
直到所有人惊喜地叫道：
“那花多美啊！”

（阿尔弗雷德·丁尼生）

Pippa's Song

The year's at the spring,
And day's at the morn,
Morning's at the seven;
The hill-top's dew-pearled;
The lark's on the wing;
The snail's on the thorn;
God's in his heaven——
All's right with the world.

(Rorbert Browning)

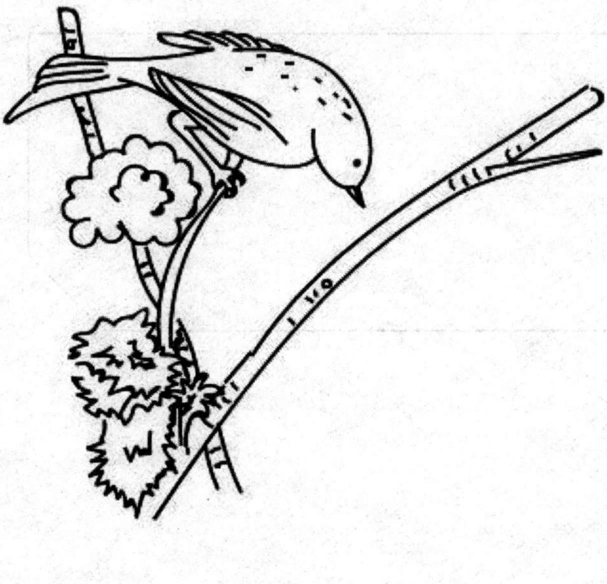

译文

比芭之歌

岁在新春，
日值清晨，
旭日东升；
山坡露珠晶莹；
晴空云雀飞行；
蜗牛窝在荆棘丛；
上帝则在天堂中——
世间万事清平。

（罗伯特·勃朗宁）

练习

抄写这首诗。

Chapter 4

Fables and Fairy Tales | 寓言和童话

The North Wind and the Sun

Mr. North Wind was out early one morning. He blew the trees until he almost broke their tops. He blew the dust on the road, so that it made big clouds. He blew the corn and the clover blossoms right down on the ground.

"Who is so strong as I?" he sang.

"I am," said the Sun, as he came out from a cloud. "I am as strong as you, and still stronger."

"Let us see which is the stronger," said Mr. Wind. "There comes a man that has on a thick cloak. Let us try to take it off."

Mr. Wind tried first. He blew as hard as he could. But the man only drew his cloak close about him, and Mr. Wind could not take it off.

Then the Sun tried. He made the air warm, and sent his beams down on the man.

At once the man took off his cloak. "How pleasant the sun feels," he said, "after that fierce wind."

(Aesop, adapted)

译文

北风和太阳

一天清晨，北风先生早早就出了门，他把大树的树顶都吹折了，吹得地上的泥土都扬了起来，远远看上去像乌云一样，吹得玉米和苜蓿都把头垂到了地上。

“有谁能和我一样厉害？”他唱道。

“我，”太阳说着，从乌云中走了出来，“我和你一样厉害，甚至比你还要厉害。”

“那我们就来看看谁更厉害吧。”北风先生说道，“看那边走来一个人，他穿着一件斗篷，我们看看谁能把他的斗篷脱掉吧。”

北风先生先来试了一试。他用尽力气吹。但是那个人却把斗篷裹得越来越紧，于是北风先生没能脱掉那个人的斗篷。

接着，太阳也来试试看。他把到处都晒得暖洋洋的，把光芒洒到那个人身上。

那个人立刻脱下了外套。“这阳光多令人愉悦呀，”那个人说道，“尤其是在狂风之后。”

（伊索，有删改）

练习

写出下列单词的同类别的词语：as, tree, corn。

as ______________________

tree ______________________

corn ______________________

Timothy's Shoes

Timothy was often late for school and late for dinner.

"It is time for him to put on the fairy shoes," said his mother.

"Now, Tim," said she, "I want you to be a good boy. And take care that you do not stay away from school or be late. If you do, these shoes will pinch you."

Timothy put on the shoes. Once or twice on the way to school he stopped to pick flowers. But the shoes pinched him, and he ran on.

When the path ran near the swamp, he looked down and saw the golden buttercups.

Then he tossed away his books. Buttercups he must have.

As soon as Timothy turned to the flowers, the shoes wanted to go to the school. In a short time the wet mud pulled them off his feet.

Timothy was glad to be rid of them. He waded about and picked buttercups, until he hurt his foot on a stone. Then he went on to school.

In the school-room, just at Tim's place in class, were the little shoes. There was mud all over them, and there was a buttercup in each one.

"You have been in the swamp, Timothy," said the

teacher. "Put on your shoes."

Timothy had to go to the foot of the class. The shoes did not like to stay there. So they pinched his poor feet, until Timothy pulled them off.

The shoes then pattered back to their old place near the head. There they stayed, and waited for the little boy to work up to them.

Every day the shoes were in the place that Timothy should have filled. So as long as he stayed down in class, he had to stand in his socks.

In this way the shoes were of great use to Timothy. Little by Little, with their help, he left off his bad habits, until at last they did not need to pinch him at all.

(Juliana H. Ewing)

译文

蒂莫西的鞋子

蒂莫西上学迟到，吃晚餐也迟到。

“现在得让他穿上这双神奇的小鞋子了。”他的妈妈心想。

“蒂姆，我希望你能做一个好孩子。现在起你要注意了，不能逃学也不能迟到，否则，这双鞋会夹你的脚，惩罚你。”妈妈对蒂莫西说道。

于是，蒂莫西穿上了这双鞋。有这么一两回，他在上学途中停了下来，想摘几朵花，但鞋子马上就会夹他的脚，没办法，他只能继续赶路。

当蒂莫西沿着小路走到了一片泥塘，他低下头，看到这里长了些金凤花。

他立刻把书丢到了一旁，他心想：无论如何，我一定要摘到金凤花！

蒂莫西朝花丛走过去的时候，鞋子立刻往学校跑去，结果不一会儿，蒂莫西就没了鞋子，双脚沾满了泥巴。

摆脱了这双鞋，蒂莫西别提多高兴了。他趟过泥塘去摘金凤花，直到脚被石子弄伤，他才停下来，然后继续往学校走去。

教室里蒂莫西的座位上，有一双小小的鞋子，鞋子上满是泥巴，每只鞋里还放了朵金凤花。

“蒂莫西，看来你刚刚是去了泥塘。”老师说道，“把鞋子穿上。”

蒂莫西不得不穿着鞋子上课。但这双鞋好像不喜欢蒂莫西的脚，他一穿上鞋，鞋子就夹他的脚，直到蒂莫西把鞋子脱下来才作罢。

然后鞋子踏着轻快的步子回到了它之前待的地方——最靠前的位

置。鞋子就在那里待着，等着小家伙蒂莫西追上它。

鞋子每天都待在蒂莫西的位置上。所以只要蒂莫西去上课，他就得站着，脚上只有袜子。

就这样，这双鞋在蒂莫西的生活中发挥了重要的作用。在它的帮助下，蒂莫西一点点地改掉了从前的坏习惯，到最后，这双鞋再也不需要夹蒂莫西的脚来惩罚他了。

（朱莉安娜·霍雷希克·尤因）

作者简介

朱莉安娜·霍雷希克·尤因，简称尤因夫人，英国维多利亚时代末期儿童文学女作家。

The Lady-Bird and the Fly(1)

预习

broom /bruːm/ 扫帚

burnt /bɜːrnt/ 烧伤

cook /kʊk/ 烹饪

creak /kriːk/ 发出嘎吱声

herself /hɜːrˈself/ 她自己

sweep /swiːp/ 扫

together /təˈgeðər/ 一起

A lady-bird and a fly once kept house together. They cooked their food in an egg-shell.

One day the lady-bird fell in and burnt herself. The fly set up so loud a cry, that the little door of the room asked, "Why do you cry?" "Because the lady-bird has burnt herself," said the fly.

The door began to creak. "Why are you creaking?" asked the broom.

"Shall I not creak?
Lady-bird is burnt,
And little fly weeps."

The broom began to sweep the floor as hard as it could.

A little cart went past the door, and saw the dust.

"Why are you sweeping so hard, broom?" said the cart.

"Shall I not sweep?
Lady-bird is burnt,
Little fly weeps,
Little door creaks,
Little broom sweeps."

The cart began to run. "Why are you running so?" asked the ash-heap.

"Shall I not run?" said the cart,
When Lady-bird is burnt,
Little fly weeps,
Little door creaks,
And little broom sweeps,
While little cart runs."

(Jacob and Wilhelm Grimm)

译文

瓢虫和苍蝇（1）

一只瓢虫和一只苍蝇一起生活。他们常常在一只鸡蛋壳里煮饭。

有一天，瓢虫不小心掉进了蛋壳，烫伤了。看到自己朋友受伤，小苍蝇伤心地大哭起来。房门问他：“你为什么哭呀？”“因为瓢虫烧伤了。”小苍蝇回答道。

于是，房门开始嘎吱作响。“你为什么一直嘎吱作响呀？”小扫帚问道。

“难道我不该嘎吱作响吗？

瓢虫烧伤了，

苍蝇也哭了。”

于是，小扫帚开始用力扫地，使出了最大的力气。

小推车从门前经过，看到了屋子里尘土飞扬的样子。

“小扫帚，你为什么要这么用力扫地呀？”小推车问道。

“难道我不该扫地吗？

瓢虫烧伤了，

苍蝇也哭了，

门嘎吱作响了，

小扫帚就扫地了。”

于是，小推车跑了起来。“你为什么跑得这么快呀？”灰烬问道。

“难道我不该快跑吗？”

瓢虫受伤了，

苍蝇哭泣了，
门嘎吱作响了，
小扫帚扫地了，
小推车就奔跑起来了。”

（格林兄弟）

The Lady-Bird and the Fly(2)

The ash-heap began to burn. "Why do you burn?" asked a tree that grew near.

"I must burn," said the ash-heap,

"For lady-bird is burnt,

And little fly weeps,

Little door creaks,

Little broom sweeps,

And little cart runs."

"So will I rustle," said the little tree; and is shook so much that the leaves fell off.

Some leaves fell into the spring. "Why do you rustle?" asked the spring.

"Shall I not rustle?" said the tree.

"Lady-bird is burnt,

Little fly weeps,

Little door creaks,

Little broom sweeps,

Little cart runs,

And little fire burns."

"Little fire shall not burn," said the spring. "I will show you what to do."

Then the spring began

to flow, and put out the fire. The cart saw it, and stopped its wheels. The broom went and stood in the corner. The door closed. The fly dried he eyes. And the lady-bird went on with her cooking.

(Jacob and Wilhelm Grimm)

译文

瓢虫和苍蝇（2）

于是，灰烬开始燃烧了。“你为什么烧起来了？”旁边的小树问道。

“我必须燃烧呀，”灰烬说，

“因为瓢虫烧伤了，

小苍蝇哭泣了，

小门嘎吱作响了，

小扫帚扫地了，

小推车也奔跑起来了。”

“那么我要用力摇摆。”小树说道。于是小树开始剧烈地晃动，树叶都晃掉了。

有些叶子落到了泉水里，“你为什么要用力地摇摆呀？”清泉问道。

“难道我不该摇摆吗？”小树说，

“瓢虫烧伤了，

小苍蝇哭泣了，

小门嘎吱作响了，

小扫帚扫地了，

小推车奔跑了，

小火苗也燃烧了。”

“小火苗不该烧起来。”泉水说，“看我的。”

于是，清泉涌了过来，浇灭

了火苗。小推车看到火被浇灭了，就停下了轮子。小扫帚则回到了角落，安静了下来。门关上了，小苍蝇擦干了眼泪，而瓢虫又开始做她的美味佳肴了。

（格林兄弟）

练习

写出故事里所有表示动作的单词，如“run”等。

The Strongest——Who? Or Which?(1)

预习

against /əˈgenst/ 对着

bridge /brɪdʒ/ 桥

froze /froʊz/ 冻着

half /hæf/ 一半

mountain /ˈmaʊntən/ 山

nothing /ˈnʌθɪŋ/ 什么都没有

skipped /skɪpt/ 跳过的

slipped /slɪpt/ 打滑的

smooth /smuːð/ 光滑的

One time in the country where you now live, there happened to be a big frost, and the pond froze over. Mr. Rabbit ran along that way, and found that the pond had a bridge of ice.

As Mr. Rabbit wished to go to the other side, he skipped over this bridge.

The ice was so smooth that when he got about half away, his feet slipped from under him and he fell.

When he got up, he began to think that the Ice must be

very strong to hit him so hard.

He said to the Ice, “You are very strong.”

“I am so,” said the Ice.

“Well, if you are so strong, how can the Sun melt you?”

The Ice said nothing, so Mr. Rabbit asked the Sun, “Are you very strong?”

“So they tell me,” said the Sun.

“Then how can the Clouds hide you?”

The Sun had nothing to say. Mr. Rabbit looked at the Clouds.

“Are you very strong?”

“We have heard so,” said the Clouds.

“How can the Wind blow you?”

The Clouds sailed away, and Mr. Rabbit asked the Wind, “Are you very strong?”

“To be sure,” said the Wind.

“Then how can the Mountain stand against you?”

The wind blew itself away, and then Mr. Rabbit asked the Mountain, “Are you very strong?”

“So it seems,” said the Mountain.

“How can the Mouse make a nest in you?”

The Mountain did not say anything.

(Joel Chandler Harris)

译文

到底谁最厉害？（1）

你们现在生活的这座城市，曾经经历过一次大霜冻，池塘全都结了冰。兔子先生沿着池塘向前走，忽然发现池塘上架起了一座冰桥。

因为兔子先生想去池塘的另一边，便决定从这座冰桥上跳过去。

但是冰面特别滑，结果走到一半的时候，可怜的兔子先生就滑倒了。

等到他从冰面上站起来的时候，他觉得冰肯定特别厉害，不然怎么会把他摔得这么疼呢。

于是，兔子先生就对冰说："你真厉害！"

"我是很厉害。"冰答道。

"可是，如果你真的那么厉害，那为什么太阳能把你晒化呢？"

冰不说话了，于是兔子先生跑去问太阳："你很厉害吗？"

"他们是这么跟我说的。"太阳说。

"那为什么云彩能把你挡住？"

太阳也无话可说了。兔子先生便望向云彩。

"你们很厉害吗？"

"有人那么说过。"云彩回答道。

"那为什么风能把你们吹散？"

云彩默默飞走了，而兔子先生继续问风："你很厉害吗？"

"那是自然！"风答道。

“那为什么无论你怎么吹，山都能屹立不倒？”

风悄悄溜走了，然后兔子先生问山：“你很厉害吗？”

“好像是这样。”山说。

“那老鼠为什么能在你身上打洞？”

山只能沉默不语了。

（乔尔·钱德勒·哈里斯）

The Strongest——Who? Or Which?(2)

So Mr. Rabbit asked the Mouse, "Are you very strong?"

"Oh, yes," said the Mouse.

"How can the Cat catch you?"

The Mouse hid in the grass. Mr. Rabbit asked the Cat, "Are you very strong?"

"Yes, indeed," said the Cat.

"How can the Dog chase you?"

The Cat began to wash her face. Then Mr. Rabbit asked the Dog, "Are you very strong?"

"Oh, very strong," said the Dog.

"Then why does the Stick scare you?"

The Dog did not answer, and Mr. Rabbit asked the Stick, "Are you very strong?"

"Everybody says so."

"Then how can the Fire burn you?"

The Stick was dumb, and Mr. Rabbit asked the Fire, "Are you very strong?"

"Anybody will tell you so," the Fire answered.

"How can the Water quench you?"

The Fire hid behind the Smoke. Then Mr. Rabbit asked the Water, "Are you very strong?"

"Strong is no name for it," answered the Water.

"How can the Ice cover you?"

The Water went running down the River. After it had gone, the Ice said to Mr. Rabbit, "You see that you had to come back to me at last."

"Yes," said Mr. Rabbit, "and now I am going away. You are too much for me." Then Mr. Rabbit hopped off, rubbing his bruises.

(Joel Chandler Harris)

译文

到底谁最厉害？（2）

于是兔子先生跑去问老鼠："你很厉害吗？"

"当然啦。"老鼠说道。

"那为什么猫还能抓住你？"

老鼠立刻躲进了草丛。兔子先生又去问猫："你很厉害吗？"

"是啊，当然啦。"猫答道。

"那狗为什么能追得你上蹿下跳？"

猫只能假装若无其事地洗脸。然后兔子先生又去找狗："你很厉害吗？"

"是，非常厉害。"狗说。

"那为什么一根手杖就能把你吓跑？"

狗答不上来了，于是兔子先生又去问手杖："你很厉害吗？"

"大家都这么说。"

"那为什么一把火就能把你烧掉？"

手杖沉默了，兔子先生接着去问火："你很厉害吗？"

"任何人都会这么跟你说。"火回答道。

"那为什么水能把你浇灭？"

听了这话，火就藏到烟的后面去了。然后兔子先生又去问水："你很厉害吗？"

“厉害这个词说的就是我。”水答道。

“那冰为什么能盖住你？”

水不声不响地流进了河里。等它走后，冰对兔子先生说：“你看，你最后还是回到我这了。”

“是啊，”兔子先生说道，“现在我要走了，我没法承受你的威力啊！”兔子先生摸摸了身上的淤青，然后匆匆离开了。

（乔尔·钱德勒·哈里斯）

练习

1. 抄下故事里所有和兔子先生说过话的角色的名字。
2. 这些名字的首字母都有什么样的特点？
3. 问问你的老师，让他告诉你为什么这些字母要这样使用。

The Mallard Ducks

"I feel a warm breeze from the north this morning," said Mr. Mallard. "It moves all my feathers. We must soon set out for our home in the mountains."

"Why not stay here?" asked Mrs. Mallard. "I like Mississippi. It is just as good a place to live in as those Tennessee mountains."

"My dear, this does well enough for winter, but it is not a fit summer home for ducks."

When they had gone a long way, they came to a fine country. Then they made a nest by pulling together a little dry grass and some leaves.

In this nest Mrs. Mallard laid ten beautiful blue eggs. Every day she picked soft down from her breast and put it into the nest.

The eggs were quite cozy in their feather bed. Mrs. Mallard sat upon them all the time to keep them warm.

Before very long there were nine little down ducks in the nest. Mr. and Mrs. Mallard were very proud of them. They took the little ones to the water, and taught them to swim. When November came, the ducks all said, "Quack! Quack! Away! Away!" Then the whole flock flew to the South to spend the winter in the rice fields.

(Eva Williams Malone, adapted)

译文

野鸭子

“今天早上的北风很温暖，”野鸭子先生说道，“我的每根羽毛都感觉到了。我们必须马上动身，回到山上的家里去。”

“为什么不待在这呢？”野鸭子太太问道，“我喜欢密西西比，和田纳西的那些山一样，这里住着也很舒服啊。”

“亲爱的，冬天这里的确是个好地方，但是夏天，对我们鸭子来说，就不一定了。”

在经过长途飞行之后，他们来到了美丽的乡村。然后他们揪了一些干草和树叶，筑了个窝。

野鸭子太太在窝里生了十枚美丽的青色鸭蛋。每天，她都从胸脯上拔下一些柔软的羽毛垫在窝里。

鸭蛋们待在他们的羽毛床上，可舒服了。野鸭子太太每天都一直坐在鸭蛋上，给他们保暖。

不久之后，鸭窝里多了九只小鸭子，野鸭子夫妇感到非常骄傲。他们把小家伙们带到水里，教他们怎么游泳。

十一月来了，所有的鸭子们都说：“呱呱，呱呱，走吧，走吧。”于是整个鸭群都飞到了南方的稻田里过冬去了。

（伊娃·威廉姆斯·马隆，有删改）

练习

将下列句子改成单数形式。

The clouds hide you.

The _______ hides you.

The squirrels are working.

The _______ is working.

The carts run.

The _______ runs.

The Three Bears(1)

Tiny Bear: Mother, mother, Jack Frost has been in the woods, and the chestnuts are falling out of the burrs this morning! May I go out and gather some?

Middle-Sized Bear: Just in a moment, Tiny. As soon as I have made the pudding, your father and I will go with you. Now bring three bowls from the shelf. I will put the pudding in to cool.

Tiny Bear: Here is the huge bowl for Father, here is the middle-sized bowl for you, and here is the tiny one for me.

Middle-Sized Bear: Thank you. I am ready. Tell your father.

Huge Bear: I must brush my coat first. Farmer White's apple tree always makes my fur rough, and I was in his orchard so late last night, that I could not see to brush my coat when I came home.

[Just after the bear leave the house, Golden-hair comes in.]

Golden-hair: What a pretty house! It looks like a play house. I wonder who lives here.

Nobody answers my rap. Can any one live here? I shall look in the keyhole.

I do not see any one. I shall turn the knob just a little. Oh, the door is not locked. I shall go in. Oh, this is a beautiful house!

There is some pudding on the table. How hungry I am! I shall eat some out of this huge bowl. Ah, it is too hot! I shall taste this in the middle-sized bowl. No, I do not like this. It is too cold.

Oh, here is a tiny bowl! I think this will do. How good it is! It is neither too hot nor too cold. There, I have eaten it all up. It was just enough. Now I shall sit down in this huge chair and take a rest. That is too hard. I shall try this middle-sized chair. No, it is too soft.

Here is a tiny chair that is just the right size. I shall sit in it. How nice it is! Oh, oh, oh! The seat has come out. It is a wonder that I was not hurt.

(Classic Story)

译文

三只熊的故事（1）

小小熊：爸爸，妈妈，严寒已经到森林来了，今天早上栗子的毛刺也掉落了！我能出去收集些回来吗？

妈妈熊：等一会儿，小家伙。等我做好布丁，我和你爸爸就跟你一起去。现在先去架子上拿三个碗过来，我好把布丁放进去凉一凉。

小小熊：这个大碗给爸爸，这个不大不小的碗给你，还有这个小的给我。

妈妈熊：谢谢，我做好了。去告诉爸爸吧。

爸爸熊：我要先把外套刷一下。农夫怀特家的苹果树把我的一身毛都弄得不光滑了，昨晚我很晚才离开他的果园，等回家想刷外套的时候天已经黑得看不清了。

[就在小熊一家都出门后，金发小姑娘走过来。]

金发小姑娘：多可爱的房子啊！看起来像是过家家一样。真想知道谁住在这儿。

我敲门，没人回答。有人住在这吗？我应该透过钥匙孔看看。

没看见人呀。我应该扭一下把手看看。噢，门没锁。我应该进去看看。噢，这个房子真漂亮啊！

桌子上有一些布丁。我好饿呀！我应该吃点这个大碗里的，啊哦，这个太烫了！那我再尝尝这个中等大小的碗里的。哦不，我不喜欢这个。这个太冷了。

喔，这个还有个小碗！这个也许不错。真好吃！不是太冷也不是太热。好啦，我全吃完了。这足够了。现在我要在这把大椅子上坐着休息一会。不，这太硬了。我再试试这把中等大小的椅子。不，这太软了。

这儿还有个小椅子刚刚好大小。我坐进去试试。真舒服！摇啊摇，摇啊摇，啊呀！椅子坏了，我没摔伤真是个奇迹。

（经典故事）

The Three Bears(2)

预习

bolster /ˈboʊlstər/ 长枕头

perhaps /pərˈhæps/ 或许

pillow /ˈpɪloʊ/ 枕头

somebody /ˈsʌmbədi/ 某个人

spoon /spuːn/ 勺子

Golden-hair: I am sleepy. I shall go up-stairs. Perhaps there are beds up there. What fun to climb up into this huge one! Oh, I can't sleep here! The bolster is too hard for me.

The middle-sized bed will be better. Yes, the pillow is just right, but the bed is too soft for me.

What a dear little bed! It is just right, so I shall take a good sleep.

[As soon as Golden-hair falls asleep, the three bears come in.]

Huge Bear: Here is a spoon in my bowl. somebody has been at my pudding.

Middle-Sized Bear: Here is a spoon in my bowl. Somebody has been at my pudding.

Tiny Bear: Oh, here a spoon in my bowl! Somebody has been at my pudding, and has eat it all up.

Huge Bear: We must find out who has been here. Let us sit down and rest. Oh, somebody has been sitting in my chair!

Middle-sized Bear: Somebody has been sitting in my chair!

Tiny Bear: Somebody has been sitting in my chair, and has sat the bottom of it out!

Huge Bear: There must be somebody in our house. Let us go upstairs and look. Oh, somebody has been lying in my bed, and pulled the bolster out of place.

Middle-Sized Bear: Somebody has been lying in my bed, and pulled the pillow out of place.

Tiny Bear: Somebody has been lying in my bed,—and here she is. Oh, oh, oh! It's a little girl. She sprang right out of the window. You can catch her, father!

Huge Bear: No, we'll let her run away. Oh, that is Farmer White's little Golden-hair. We must not touch her at all.

This is Farmer White's wood. If anything happened to Golden-hair, Farmer John would bring his gun, and drive us away, far from his apples and honey.

(Classic Story)

译文

三只熊的故事（2）

金发小姑娘：我困了，我应该上楼看看。也许楼上会有床。爬上这张大床真有意思啊！哦不，我不能睡这！床板太硬了。

那个中等大小的床会好点吧。没错，这个枕头刚刚好，但对我来说床太软了。

哎呀，这个小床！正好，这样我就能睡个好觉了。

[金发小姑娘一睡着，小熊一家就回来了。]

爸爸熊：我的碗里有个勺子。有人动过我的布丁了。

妈妈熊：我的碗里有个勺子。有人动过我的布丁了。

小小熊：哦，我的碗里也有个勺子！有人动过我的布丁，还全给吃光了。

爸爸熊：我们需要找到谁来过这。都坐下休息一会吧。啊，有人坐过我的椅子！

妈妈熊：我的椅子也有人坐过！

小小熊：我的椅子也被人坐过，还把椅子底儿坐坏了！

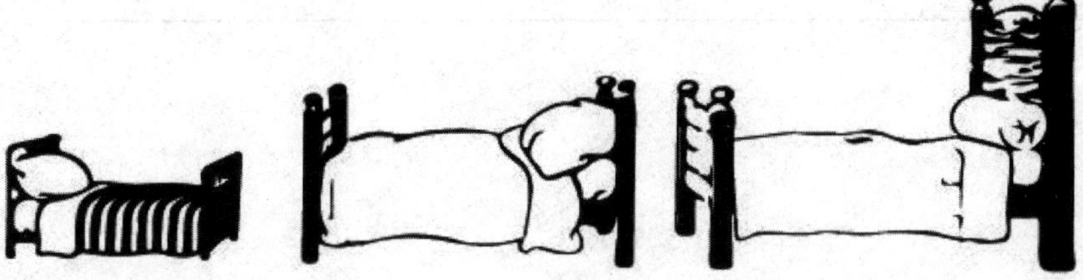

爸爸熊：房子里一定还有别人。咱们上楼看看。噢，有人睡过我的床，还把垫枕弄乱了。

妈妈熊：我的床也有人睡过，还把枕头弄乱了。

小小熊：我的床也被人睡过。她还在这儿，啊，啊，啊！是个小女孩。她从窗户跳出去了，把她抓住，爸爸！

大熊：不，让她逃走吧。哦，那是农夫怀特家的金发小姑娘。我们可不能伤害她。

这是农夫怀特家的树林。要是金发小姑娘出了什么意外，农夫约翰就会带着他的枪，把我们赶走，我们就没法接近他的苹果和蜂蜜啦。

（经典故事）

练习

从第一个月开始，写下一年所有月份的名称。

David's Trip to the Moon

David looked up. The moon had not risen any farther out of the water. There it hung above the edge of the world. It was almost round and almost full, like a great bubble of brightness.

David next found himself running across what seemed to be sparkling silver grass. Everything shone around him, and he felt the light rise up against his eyes and face.

He felt so happy that he did not know what to do. He skipped and played just as a lamb skips and plays on the grass.

It seemed to David as though the moon was coming toward him. It seemed to grow bigger and bigger, but he was only getting closer and closer to the moon. It was no longer like a bubble. It was a great round globe of light.

Almost before he knew it, David was at the edge of the world. And there was the moon rising above him as big as a church. He stood quite still and looked up at it.

Click-clock! What was that? A half-door opened, and there stood a little old man. He was as gray as the evening.He had long white hair and queer clothes. His face was covered all over with cobwebs of silver wrinkles. It was the Man-in-the-moon, and he was smoking a long pipe of tobacco.

"How do you do, David?" said he. "Will you come in?"

"Yes," said David, "I should like to."

"That is good," said the Man-in-the-moon. And he opened the other half of the door. "Now! Give me your hand."

The Man-in-the-moon reached down to David, and David reached up to the Man-in-the-moon. "Now, then! A long step," said the Man-in-the-moon. And there was David in the door-way of the moon-house.

Then the moon rose slowly, slowly, up into the sky and floated away. And the Man-in-the-moon shut the door, click-clock!

(Howard Pyle, adapted)

译文

大卫的月亮之旅

大卫仰望夜空，看到月亮悬在水面上，在世界的边缘，维持着不变的高度。那晚的月亮又大又圆，就像色彩明亮的大泡泡一般。

随后，大卫发现自己在一片草坪上奔跑，银色的草坪看起来闪闪发光，身边的一切都在闪烁着，他感到了一束光照向他的眼睛和脸颊。

大卫高兴得不知所措，他蹦蹦跳跳的，如同在草原上撒欢的小羊。

月亮好像正朝他飘过来，变得越变越大，他也离月亮越来越近。此时，月亮已经不像泡泡了，而是一个巨大圆球，散发着光芒。

还没等大卫反应过来，他就来到了世界的边缘，像一座教堂这么大的月亮在他眼前升了起来，他静静地抬头仰望。

钟声响了起来。那是怎么回事？半边门打开了，一个身材矮小的老男人站在那儿，他的肤色和夜晚一样，是灰色的。他的脸上布满了蜘蛛网一般的银色皱纹，有一头白色的长发，穿着怪异。他，就是生活在月亮上的人。他吸着一根长长的烟管。

“你好，大卫。”他说道，“你要进来吗？”

“好的，”大卫说道，“我很荣幸。”

“太好了，”这位月中人说，他把另一半门也打开了，“那么现在，把你的手给我。”

月中人向大卫伸手，大卫牵到了他的手。“现在，我们要走一段长长的台阶。”月中人说道。此时，大卫已经来到了月亮之屋的门口。

月亮缓缓上升，进入云层，慢慢飘走了。月中人关上了门，钟声再次响了起来！

（霍华德·派尔，有删改）

David's Work in the Moon

"Come, David," said the Man-in-the-moon, "it is time for your work now. Tomorrow night you shall see something new."

Then the Man-in-the-moon led David up to the third story of the moon-house. There was nothing above him but the hollow sky.

The first thing that David saw was a great basket full of stars of all kinds. Some shone white, and some blue, and some rosy red. The light shone from them, so that all about was a mist of brightness.

Beside the basket was a bundle of lamb's wool.

"There is your work," said the Man-in-the-moon. "It is to polish the stars with lamb's wool, so that they may shine brightly when the moon wanes, and the sky is dark once more."

David sat down on the wooden bench, and took up a big star. He blew his breath upon it, and rubbed it with lamb's wool. As he robbed, the star grew brighter and brighter, and glowed with light as though it were alive.

David did not know how beautiful a star could be until he held it in his own hand and rubbed it with lamb's wool.

I dare say that there are some wise folk who will tell you that this is all nonsense. All that you have to do then is to look up into the sky when the moon is full.

There you will see for yourself that there are hardly any stars to be seen. Those few are so dull and dim that they hardly twinkle at all.

That is because somebody in the moon is polishing the others with lamb's wool to make them bright for the time when the sky is dark again.

(Howard Pyle, adapted)

译文

大卫在月球上的工作

“来吧，大卫，”月中人说，“现在你该工作了。明晚，你就能看到不一样的世界。”

于是，月中人带大卫来到了月亮之屋的三楼，头顶上只有空荡荡的天空。

大卫第一眼看到的是一个篮子，里面装着各种各样的星星，有的闪着白光，有的闪着蓝光，有的闪着玫瑰红色的光，所有的星星都闪烁着，整个篮子散发出朦胧的光芒。

篮子的旁边有一捆羊毛。

“这就是你的工作，”月亮老爷爷说道，“用羊毛把星星擦亮，这样下次月亮渐缺，天色渐黑的时候，星星就会闪闪发光。”

大卫坐在木凳上，拿起一颗大星星，轻轻吹一口气，再用羊毛擦一擦。星星越擦越亮，还发光散热，如同一个鲜活的生命一般。

大卫握着一颗星星，用羊毛把它擦亮，而在这之前他根本不知道星星是那么美。

我敢说，一些自作聪明的人会告诉你，这些故事都是瞎编的。但你只需在满月的时候，抬头望望天空。

你会发现，天空上的星星寥寥无几，仅有的几颗星星也黯淡无光，更别说闪耀发光了。

这是因为在月亮上，有人正在擦拭着其他的星星，只为在第二天夜幕降临时，让大家看到耀眼的星光。

（霍华德·派尔，有删改）

练习

填空（注意词语的复数形式）。

The beaver builds dams.

The beavers _____ dams.

The owl hoots.

The owls _____ hoots.

The tree makes leaves.

The trees _____ leaves.

The leopard eats chickens.

The leopards _____ chickens.

The hear likes chestnuts.

The bears _____ chestnuts.

The wrens know the place.

The wren _____ the place.

The cardinals are red.

The cardinal _____ red.

The blue jays steal.

The blue jay _____.

The bees sting.

The bee _____ .

The Blue Hen's Chicken(1)

预习

caused /kɔːzd/ 使发生

creeping /ˈkriːpɪŋ/ 爬行的

fretted /ˈfretɪd/ 焦躁的

hatched /ˈhætʃt/ 孵化的

real /ˈriːəl/ 真实的

tenth /tenθ/ 第十个

waddle /ˈwɑːdl/ 摇摇摆摆地走

Mrs. Duck was the very one that caused Mrs. Blue hen all the trouble. While wading in the stream, Mrs. Duck had seen Mrs. Blue Hen going to her nest for three days, slipping and creeping through the bushes.

On the third day, Mrs. Duck did some slipping and creeping herself. She crept up close enough to see Mrs. Blue Hen when she ran away cackling.

Then Mrs. Duck waddled up and peeped into the nest. "I knew that she must be mighty proud, the stuck-up thing! I can see that by the way she steps around here. Quack, quack! Quack, quack!"

Then and there Mrs. Duck, all muddy as she was, got into Mrs. Blue Hen's nest, and sat on her beautiful white eggs. Besides, Mrs. Duck laid one of her own dull-looking eggs in Mrs. Blue Hen's nest. And that was the real cause of all the trouble.

When Mrs. Blue Hen had ten eggs in the nest, she went to sitting. After three weeks, nine little chickens were hatched. She was very proud of them.

She taught them how to talk, and then she wanted to get off her nest and teach them how to scratch about and earn their own living. But there was still one egg to hatch, and so Mrs. Blue Hen kept on sitting on it.

Mrs. Blue Hen fretted a good deal, but in another week the tenth egg hatched. She felt much better after this. Indeed, she was very comfortable. She did not even take the trouble to look at the chicken that hatched from the tenth egg.

(Joel Chandler Harris)

译文

蓝母鸡的小鸡（1）

蓝母鸡太太身上一切麻烦，都是鸭子太太这个罪魁祸首惹来的。鸭子太太在小溪游泳时，看见了蓝母鸡太太藏在灌木丛里的巢，连续三天，蓝母鸡太太都鬼鬼祟祟地去了那里。

在第三天的时候，鸭子太太也鬼鬼祟祟地去了那个巢。她蹑手蹑脚地靠近，看见蓝母鸡太太“咯咯”叫着走了。

鸭子太太便摇摇摆摆地走过去，窥视着这个巢。“我知道她一定得意极了，那个趾高气扬的家伙！我甚至能想到她走在这里的样子！嘎！嘎！嘎！嘎！”

于是，鸭子太太在自己身上涂满泥巴，往巢里一坐，屁股落在了蓝母鸡太太漂亮的白色鸡蛋上。然后，她往巢里下了一个样子粗笨的鸭蛋。这个鸭蛋，正是一切麻烦的真正源头。

当巢里有了十个蛋后，蓝母鸡太太开始坐着孵蛋了。过了三个星期，九只小鸡破壳出来了，她感到自豪极了。

她教他们说话，后来，她也很想从巢里出来，教他们在地里刨出果腹的食物。但是，巢里还有一颗蛋没有孵出来，她得继续坐在那儿。

蓝母鸡太太非常焦虑。又过了一周，第十个蛋孵出来，她才感觉好多了，心情十分舒畅，甚至没有费神去看刚孵出来的小鸡长什么样。

（乔尔 · 钱德勒 · 哈里斯）

The Blue Hen's Chicken(2)

But when she brought her children off the nest, it was a great surprise to her to find that one of them was not at all like the rest. Nine of her children were as neat looking as she could wish them to be, but the tenth one was a sight to see.

This poor child had weak eyes, a broad bill, and big flat feet. Its feet were so big that it waddled when it walked, and all the toes of each foot were joined together.

Mrs. Blue Hen felt very bad, and kept her children hidden as long as she could. But she had to come out after a while. When she did, there was a noise in the barnyard.

The old white hen was the first to begin it. "Look-look-look!" she cried out, "Look at the Blue Hen's chickens!"

Then the guinea hens began to laugh, and the old turkey thought that it was very funny.

Mrs. Blue Hen hung her head, and carried her children away off in the woods.

But her flat-footed chicken was the cause of so much talk, that it became a by-word in all that country. When any stranger came along looking rough and ragged, people always said that he was the Blue Hen's chicken.

(Joel Chandler Harris)

译文

蓝母鸡的小鸡（2）

直到蓝母鸡把孩子们带出巢里，她才发现有个孩子和其他九个长得完全不一样，蓝母鸡惊呆了。这九个孩子都和她预料中一样可爱，但剩下那个，根本就是截然不同的模样。

这可怜的孩子不但看不清东西，还有一张宽宽的嘴巴、一双扁平的大脚，走路时还摇摇晃晃的。而且，他所有的脚趾都连在一起了。

蓝母鸡太太心情非常低落，她想尽可能晚点把孩子们带出去，但过不了多久，她还是得出门。她一出现在晒谷场，说闲话的就来了。

白色老母鸡是最先开始的。“瞧瞧！瞧瞧！”她叫道，“瞧瞧蓝母鸡的小鸡仔们！”

然后，雌珍珠鸡发出了大笑声，老火鸡也感到十分好笑。

蓝母鸡昂着头，带着孩子们离开了这里，往森林里去了。

她那扁平足的孩子还是惹了许多闲话，成了村里热烈议论的话题。有陌生人过来粗鲁地打量他一番时，人们都会说，他是蓝母鸡的孩子。

（乔尔·钱德勒·哈里斯）

Chapter 5

Story and Adventure | 冒险奇遇和故事

The Arrow Hunt(1)

"Now Papa Brown," said Grace, as her papa got off the train, "you must think of the very best game you ever knew for us to play this afternoon."

"Yes, yes," cried Carl, "something fine for us to play on our last Saturday in the country."

"Very well," said Mr. Brown, "I have thought of a fine game, and I will show you how to play it."

When he had rested, Mr. Brown called the children, and said, "The game that I have thought of is the 'arrow hunt'. It was the game that I liked best when I was a boy."

"An arrow hunt! How do you play that game?" cried all the Brown children at once.

"This is the way. I shall take a piece of chalk and make arrows on the walk, the fence, and the trees, or on anything that I please as I walk along. This is the way that the arrows will look," and he drew an arrow on a piece of board.

"I shall go first, and in fifteen minutes you may come after me. Follow just as the arrow leads.

"At the end of the arrows, if you follow them right, you will find a big red arrow, and you may have the thing that arrow rests upon."

The fifteen minutes seemed long to wait, but by and by hey were past, and away ran the children.

(Elizabeth Flint Wade)

译文

猎箭行动（1）

“布朗爸爸，”布朗先生一下火车，格蕾丝就冲过去对他说道，“现在你必须要想一个最最棒的游戏，一个可以让我们消磨一下午的游戏！”

“对啊，对啊！”小卡尔跟着大叫道，“既然这是我们在农村的最后一个周六，我们一定要玩个痛快！”

“那好吧，”布朗先生说，“我已经想到了一个超棒的游戏，一会儿我就告诉你们怎么玩。”

休息了一会儿后，布朗先生把孩子们叫了过来，对他们说道：“我刚想到的游戏是‘猎箭行动’，这可是我小时候最喜欢玩的游戏！”

“猎箭行动！要怎么玩，要怎么玩？”几个孩子立即大叫起来。

“是这样的，我会拿一支粉笔，在路上、栅栏上、树上或其他任何一个我经过的地方标上箭头，比如这样。”说着他就在黑板上画了一个箭头。

“我会先走，等我走了十五分钟后，你们就可以出发了，记得要沿着我画的箭头走。”

“如果能顺利找到所有记号并走到终点，你们就会看到一个红色的大箭头，那个时候箭头指向的东西就归你们了。”

十五分钟的等待总算过去了，时间一到，孩子们撒腿就跑。

（伊丽莎白 · 弗林特 · 韦德）

The Arrow Hunt(2)

The children followed the arrow marks with great care. They led down the board walk and along the fence, but at the turn in the road they stopped.

It was some minutes before any one could find the next arrow. It was on the fence and pointed straight into the air.

"Oh," said Grace, "it goes up into the sky, and we can't go up there."

"I think that it goes over the fence," said Rob. And he climbed up and shouted, "Yes, here it is! Come on!"

The next arrow was on a round stone. Little Jane found it.

It was great fun hunting for the arrows. They led the children into all kinds of places. They led by the side of a brook, and then across the brook on stepping stones.

They went through a meadow, and past a field of corn. By and by they led into a pretty wood along a path that wound in and out among the trees.

All at once the children came to an open place. In the very center of the grass was spread a white cloth, and on it were cakes, and berries, and four white boxes, which looked very much like candy boxes.

In the center of the cloth were four pretty hoops and eight sticks, and on top of them was a big red arrow.

Then Mr. and Mrs. Brown stepped out of the bushes,

and Mr. Brown said, "This is the end of the arrow hunt, and here we shall have our supper."

Then, happy and hungry, they sat down to eat the good things. After supper Mrs. Brown showed the children how to play "grace-hoops", the game which she used to play when she was a little girl.

When the sun was almost down, they went home. As the children went to bed that night, they said to one another, "This was the very best day of all."

(Elizabeth Flint Wade)

译文

猎箭行动（2）

孩子们小心翼翼地跟着箭头的指示向前走。他们走过了人行道，穿过了栅栏，但走到拐角的时候，他们停下了脚步。

几个孩子找了好一会儿，才找到下一个箭头，箭头在篱笆上，指向了天空。

“哦，天啊！”格蕾丝说，“箭头指着天空，但我们没办法到天上去呀。”

“我觉得这应该意味着我们要翻过这个篱笆。”罗布说道。他翻过篱笆，一会儿就听到他的叫声：“是这里，是这里！你们快过来！”

下一个箭头在一个圆圆的石头上，简找到了它。

寻找箭头的过程充满了乐趣，孩子们跟着这些箭头，足迹遍布每一个角落。他们来到小溪边，然后踩着水里的石头，穿过了小溪。

他们还穿过了一片牧场，又穿过了一片玉米地。他们不久之后被引到了一片树林里，走过了被树木包围的小道。

突然间，孩子们走到了一片空草地，草丛的正中央放了一块白色的桌布，桌上有蛋糕、浆果和四个白色糖果盒一样的盒子。

在桌布的正中心有四个很漂亮的圆环和八根树枝，上面有一个红色的大箭头。

这时，布朗夫妇从灌木丛里走了出来，布朗先生对孩子们说道：“这里就是猎箭行动的终点了，我们要在这里吃晚餐哦。”

饥肠辘辘的孩子们听到爸爸的话很开心，然后坐了下来，一起享用桌布上的佳肴。晚餐后，布朗太太教孩子们抛圆环玩，这是她小时候常玩的游戏。

一直玩到太阳快落山，他们才回家。那天晚上，孩子们要睡觉的时候，都说这是他们最快乐的一天。

（伊丽莎白 · 弗林特 · 韦德）

The Hen That Went to Doverfield(1)

Once a hen dreamed that she must go to Doverfield or the world would come to an end.

So she jumped from her perch in the oak tree, and set out on the road.

When she had gone a bit, she met a cock.

"Good-day, Cocky Locky!" said the hen.

"Good-day, Henny Penny! Where are you going so early?" said the cock.

"Oh, I am going to Doverfield, so that the world shall not come to an end," said the hen.

"Who told you that, Henny Penny?" said the cock.

"I sat in the oak tree and dreamed it last night," said the hen.

"I will go with you!" said the cock.

So they went a long way, till they met a duck.

"Good-day, Ducky Lucky!" said the cock.

"Good-day, Cocky Locky! Where are you going so early?" said the duck.

"I am going to Doverfield, so that the world shall not come to an end," said the cock.

"Who told you that, Cocky Locky?"

"Henny Penny!" said the cock.

"Who told you that, Henny Penny?" said the duck.

"I sat in the oak and dreamed it last night," said the hen.

"I will go with you!" said the duck.

So they started again, and walked till they met a gander.

"Good-day, Gandy Pandy!" said the duck.

"Good-day, Ducky Lucky!" said the gander. "Where are you going so early?"

"I am going to Doverfield, so that the world shall not come to an end," said the duck.

"Who told you that, Ducky Lucky?" said the gander.

"Cocky Locky!"

"Who told you that, Cocky Locky?"

"Henny Penny!"

"How do you know that, Henny Penny?" said the gander.

"I sat in the oak and dreamed it last night, Gandy Pandy," said the hen.

"I will go with you!" said the gander.

(Norse Folklore)

译文

一只要去多文菲尔德的母鸡（1）

从前有一只母鸡，她晚上梦见自己必须要去多文菲尔德，否则世界就会毁灭。

于是，她从栖身的橡木树枝上跳下来，出发了。

她走了一会儿，遇到了一只公鸡。

“你好呀，公鸡洛基！”母鸡说。

“你好呀，母鸡佩妮！这么早，是要去哪儿呀？”公鸡问。

“噢！我要去多文菲尔德，不然世界就会毁灭啦。”母鸡说。

“母鸡佩妮，这是谁告诉你的？”公鸡说。

“昨晚我坐在橡树上睡觉，梦见的。”母鸡说。

“我跟你一起去！”公鸡说。

他们一起走啊走，直到遇到一只鸭子才停下来。

“你好呀，鸭子拉克！”公鸡说。

“你好呀，公鸡洛基！这么早，是要去哪儿呀？”鸭子问。

“我要去多文菲尔德，不然世界就会毁灭呀。”公鸡回答道。

“公鸡洛基，这是谁告诉你的？”

“母鸡佩妮！”公鸡说。

“母鸡佩妮，这是谁告诉你的？”鸭子问。

“昨晚我坐在橡树上睡觉，梦见的。”母鸡说。

“我跟你们一起去！”鸭子说。

于是他们再次出发，直到遇到一只公鹅才停下来。

“你好呀，公鹅潘迪！”鸭子说。

“你好呀，鸭子拉克！”公鹅说，“这么早，是要去哪儿呀？”

“我要去多文菲尔德，不然世界就会毁灭呀。”鸭子说。

“鸭子拉克，这是谁告诉你的？”公鹅问。

“公鸡洛基！”

“公鸡洛基，这是谁告诉你的？”

“母鸡佩妮！”

“母鸡佩妮，你是怎么知道的？”公鹅问。

“公鹅潘迪，这是昨晚我坐在橡树上睡觉，梦见的。”母鸡回答道。

“我跟你们一起去！”公鹅说。

（挪威民间传说）

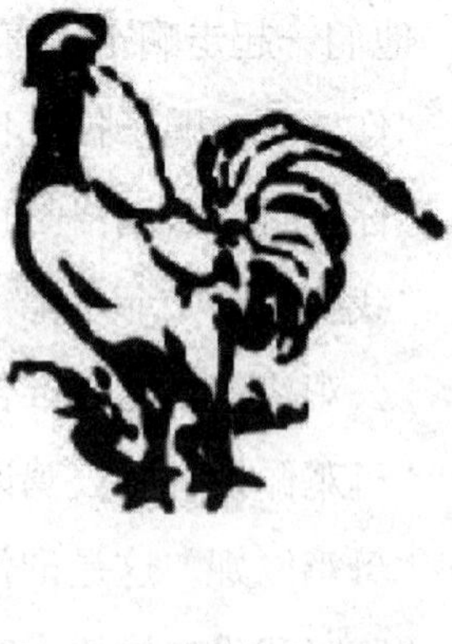

The Hen That Went to Doverfield(2)

When they had gone a bit farther, they met a fox.

"Good-day, Foxy Woxy," said the gander.

"Good-day, Gandy Pandy!"

"Where are you going, Foxy Woxy?"

"Where are you going, Gandy Pandy?"

"I am going to Doverfield, so that the world shall not come to an end," said the gander.

"Who told you that, Gandy Pandy?" said the fox.

"Ducky Lucky!"

"Who told you that, Ducky Lucky?"

"Coky Locky."

"Who told you that, Cocky Locky?"

"Henny Penny."

"How do you know that, Henny Penny?"

"I sat in the oak and dreamed last night, that if we do not go to Doverfield, the world will come to an end," said the hen.

"Oh, fie!" said the fox, "The world will not come to an end, even if you do not get there. No, come home with me to my den; that is much better, for the den is nice and cozy."

So they followed the fox home. When they came to the den, the fox put so much wood on the fire, that they all became sleepy.

The duck and the gander rested in a corner, but the cock and the hen perched on a high pole.

As soon as the gander and the duck were asleep, the fox killed them both and ate them.

The hen woke up and saw what had happened. Then she flew to a higher perch.

Soon she woke up the cock, and told him what had happened to Gandy Pandy and Ducky Lucky.

The heavy door was shut, so Cocky Locky and Henny Penny flew up through the chimney, and got away from Foxy Woxy. Then they went to Doverfield.

They always thought that if they had not gone, the world would have come to an end.

(Norse Folklore)

译文

一只要去多文菲尔德的母鸡(2)

他们又走得更远了一点，又遇到了一只狐狸。

“你好呀，狐狸沃克斯。”公鹅说。

“你好呀，公鹅潘迪！”

“狐狸沃克斯，你这是要去哪儿呀？”

“公鹅潘迪，那你又要去哪儿呢？”

“我要去多文菲尔德，不然世界就会毁灭呀。”公鹅说。

“公鹅潘迪，这是谁告诉你的？”狐狸问。

“鸭子拉克！”

“鸭子拉克，这是谁告诉你的？”

“公鸡洛基。”

“公鸡洛基，这是谁告诉你的？”

“母鸡佩妮。”

“母鸡佩妮，你是怎么知道的？”

“昨晚我坐在橡树上睡觉，梦见如果我们不去多文菲尔德，世界就会毁灭啦。”母鸡答道。

“哦，得了吧！”狐狸说，“就算你们不去那里，世界也不会毁灭的。别去了，来跟我回家吧，我的窝可好多了，又舒服又漂亮。”

于是他们跟着狐狸回家了。他们到了狐狸的窝里，狐狸把很多木材放进火堆里烧着，让温暖的火苗把他们熏得昏昏欲睡。

鸭子和公鹅待在一个角落里休息了，而公鸡和母鸡则在高处的一根杆子上栖息。

公鹅和鸭子睡熟以后，狐狸把他们都杀了，然后全部吃进了肚子里。

母鸡醒来，看到了整个经过。于是她飞到一根更高的杆子上。

她又立刻叫醒公鸡，告诉他公鹅潘迪和鸭子拉克遭遇的事情。

沉重的大门关上了，公鸡洛基和母鸡从烟囱里飞了出去，从狐狸的手里逃了出来，继续去多文菲尔德了。

他们一直坚信，如果他们不去，世界就要毁灭啦。

（挪威民间传说）

练习

1.抄写下列陈述句。

(1)The queen did not like the children.

(2)A woodpecker is tapping on the tree.

(3)Mr. North Wind was out early one morning.

(4)The fire hid behind the smoke.

2.抄写下列疑问句，或自己造几个疑问句。

(1)Who is so strong as I?

(2)Why are you sweeping so hard?”

(3)How do you play that game?

(4)Where did you get the sword?

3.在《一只要去多文菲尔德的母鸡》的故事里摘抄四个疑问句，并回答这些问句。

The Leak in the Dike

Peter had been doing an errand for his mother. She had told him to come home early. Now he was running along the dike, thinking of the nice supper that would be ready for him at home.

The dike was a great wall of stones and earth. The men had built it to keep the sea from coming over the land.

Peter could hear the waves on the other side of the wall. "You must stay on your side, old sea," he said. "If you were to flow over here, you would drown us, and wash away our houses and gardens."

The little boy knew that his father and many other men kept working at the wall all the time. This was to make it strong, so that the water could not break through.

"What is that?" Peter heard a strange sound. Then he saw that a little stream of water was pouring through the wall. In a short time it would make a big hole, and the sea would then sweep in.

He could not cover the hole with his hands. What should he do? Quickly he pulled off his coat, and held it with both hands against the hole.

Soon the water stopped running in. But it would not do for Peter to move his hands. He hoped that somebody would come. The sun went down, and all grew dark.

How cold and hungry he was! He began to think again of the warm supper at home. "I wonder if I shall die," thought Peter.

At home his mother kept watching for him. It was strange to her that he should be so late. When Peter's father came, she told him of the errand. "It is not like Peter to stay away," she said.

The father and his friends took lights, and went in search of the little boy. They did not find him that night. Early the next morning some men saw him. The brave lad was nearly frozen, but he was still in his place.

They mended the wall quickly, and carried the child home.

"Your son has saved the land!" they shouted to Peter's parents. "And God has saved your son."

(Phoebe Obey, adapted)

译文

堤坝上的裂痕

彼得帮妈妈跑腿，妈妈让他早点回家。现在，他沿着堤坝一路跑，心里惦记着家里准备好的丰盛晚餐。

堤坝是一面巨大的墙，是用石头和泥土做的。人们建造堤坝，是为了防止海水冲到陆地上来。

彼得能听到墙的另一边传来海浪声。“你必须待在你那边，大海。”他说，“要是你流到这儿来了，就会把我们淹死，把房屋和花园都冲垮。”

小男孩知道，他的父亲和很多其他男人一样，一直在这面墙上劳动。他们要加固这面墙，好让海水别把它冲垮。

“这是怎么回事？”彼得听到了一个奇怪的声音。接着，他看到墙面上涌出了一股细细的流水。很快墙面上就出现了一个大窟窿，海水直灌了进来。

他的手掌堵不住这个洞了。他应该怎么办？他迅速脱下外套，双手拿起衣服塞住了洞口。

水流止住了，但彼得也没法把双手拿开。他祈祷着有人能来。太阳渐渐西沉，天黑了下来。

他真是饥寒交迫！他又开始想象家里香喷喷的晚餐了。“真怀疑我是不是要死了。”彼得心想。

他妈妈一直在家里等着他。儿子竟然这么晚还没回来，妈妈觉得这很不寻常。彼得的爸爸回来后，她告诉他，自己让彼得跑腿去了，还说："彼得不会这么久不回来的。"

父亲和他的朋友们拿着手电筒去找这个孩子。当晚，他们一无所获。第二天清晨，有人发现了他。这个勇敢的小伙子几乎冻僵了，但他仍站在原地。

很快，他们就修好了墙，抱着孩子回了家。

"你儿子拯救了这片土地！"他们对彼得的父母欢呼道，"然后上帝拯救了你们的儿子。"

（提坦福柏·奥贝，有删改）

The Snow Baby(1)

In the winter in the far North there is no sun at all.

For four long, long months it is dark there all the time. Day and night are just the same as night is here. Only the moon and stars then give light.

The ground is covered with snow. Through this the poor deer have to dig with their hoofs for a few bites of grass and moss.

The sea is covered with ice five or six feet thick. The birds fly away, and most of the other animals go off to open water.

Only a few hungry bears and the Eskimos with their dogs are left.

The cold is so great that even the bears would freeze in an hour, if it were not for their warm fur coats. The blankets of fat under their coats also help to keep them from freezing.

Here in this strange land, in a little black house, once lived a little snow-white baby with big blue eyes.

The bed upon which the baby lay was covered with soft warm reindeer skins. The cold of the long night could not get through these skins. So the baby was always snug and warm.

When the strange people of the land heard about the white baby, they came to see her. Men, women, and children came hundreds of miles in sleighs drawn by shaggy dogs that looked like wolves.

These people are brown, with black shaggy hair, and dress in furs both in summer and winter. They wanted to touch the white baby to see if she was warm, and not made of snow.

She made friends with all the queer little brown babies sticking their heads out of their mothers' hoods.

The Eskimo babies have no cradle or anything of the kind.

They are carried all the time in great fur hoods on the backs of their mothers.

(Josephine Diebitsch Peary, adapted)

译文

雪宝宝（1）

极北之地的冬天，见不到一丝阳光。

整整四个月，这里都是一团漆黑，白天和黑夜都是这样。唯一能发光的只有星星和月亮而已。

地面上覆盖着皑皑白雪，可怜的小鹿得用蹄子去刨，才能找到一撮小草或是青苔。

海上的冰层有五六英尺（一两米）厚，鸟儿们都飞到远方去了，大多数的动物们都迁徙到了没有结冰的水域。

留在北极的，就只有饥饿的北极熊、因纽特人和他们的狗。

天气冷极了，如果北极熊没有那层厚厚的皮毛，在外面一个小时就会冻死。皮毛下那层厚厚的脂肪跟毯子似的，能帮助他们抵御严寒。

在这片神奇的土地上，曾有一个蓝眼睛、白皮肤的婴儿住在一间黑色的小屋里。

这个婴儿裹在一张床上铺着的驯鹿皮里。漫漫长夜，她就靠这张鹿皮抵御寒冷。所以她一直都温暖又舒服。

这片大陆上的人们听说她的白肤是白色的，无论男女老少，都乘着长毛狗拉的雪橇，从百里之外赶来，想看一眼这个婴儿。

这些人的皮肤都是棕色的，有着蓬松的黑发，无论冬夏，都穿着皮毛大衣。他们想摸一摸这个雪白皮肤的婴儿，看看她有没有温度，是不是雪做的。

棕色皮肤的孩子把小脑袋从母亲的斗篷里探出来，他们和白皮肤的婴儿成了好朋友。

因纽特人的宝宝们都不用摇篮之类的东西。

他们永远待在母亲的皮毛斗篷里。

（约瑟芬·迪比奇·皮尔里，有删改）

The Snow Baby(2)

At last one day the great yellow sun popped up above the tops of the mountains. It covered everything with the brightest sunlight.

The little Snow Baby was asleep when the sun first looked into the room. In a few minutes she woke up.

How the big blue eyes did open at the strange sight! How she laughed and jumped, and stretched her little hands out into the yellow light. It was the first time that she had ever seen the sun.

On every pleasant day after this she was dressed in her little fur suit, slipped into her deerskin bag, and carried out.

But she grew so fast, that very soon she was too heavy for her mother to carry.

Then some dogs and a little Eskimo sledge were brought for her. A snug box, just large enough for her to sit in, was put on the sledge.

After that the Snow Baby had a ride every day. You should have seen her team of dogs with their bright eyes, sharp ears, and big bushy tails.

They were called "Lassie" and "Lady". Sometimes they would walk along with heads team suit bushy sledge Lassie and tails up, every now and then looking round at the baby.

Then at the crack of the whip, they would dash off at a

gallop. The driver would run beside the sledge, and guide it past the rocks and lumps of ice.

The dogs always seemed to know that they were drawing a little baby, for they never tried to run away, as they often did with their Eskimo masters.

(Josephine Diebitsch Peary, adapted) .

译文

雪宝宝（2）

终于有一天，金黄的太阳爬上山顶。世间万物都镀上了一层金色的光辉。

当第一束光照进房间的时候，雪白皮肤的小宝宝还在梦中。不一会儿，她便醒了过来。

她睁大了蓝色的眼睛，看着这光芒，它可真稀奇。她跳着，笑着，伸出小小的手去抓金色的光。这是她生平第一次见到太阳。

从此，只要天气放晴，就会有人给她穿上皮毛外套，披上鹿皮斗篷，带她去户外。

但是，她长得很快，不久她的母亲就背不动她了。

于是，她出门的时候就坐着狗拉的雪橇。雪橇上有一个温暖舒适的小箱子，正好够她坐的。

自此，皮肤雪白的宝宝每天都要出门巡游。那群目光敏锐、耳朵尖尖、摇着毛茸茸的大尾巴的雪橇犬，你真应该看看。

她们的雅号不是“小姐”就是“淑女”。她们有时会兴致勃勃地跟在领头的雪橇狗后面，不时地回头看一眼婴儿。

在鞭子的呼啸声中，她们全速飞奔起来。车夫会在雪橇的旁边奔跑，引导她们避开岩石和冰块。

雪橇犬们似乎知道自己载的是一个小宝宝。她们经常从因纽特主人那里逃走，这次却从未想过要逃跑。

（约瑟芬·迪比奇·皮尔里，有删改）

Chapter 6

History and Biography | 历史传说

Sir Walter Raleigh(1)

预习

England /ˈɪŋglənd/ 英格兰

kindness /ˈkaɪndnəs/ 美德

palace /ˈpæləs/ 宫殿

people /ˈpiːpl/ 人们

return /rɪˈtɜːrn/ 返回

soil /sɔɪl/ 土壤

spread /spred/ 传播

walter /ˈwɔːltər/ （男子名）沃特

In England there lived a queen who was called "Good Queen Bess".

She tried to make her people happy, and they loved her in return.

A young man, who had heard much about her kindness, came to the palace to see her.

As he was walking to the palace, he met a lady at a place where the road was very muddy. The lady was the queen.

The young man at once took off his velvet cloak, and spread it on the ground for the queen to step on. She walked on the cloak, and so did not soil her pretty shoes.

The queen was pleased with Walter, for that was the young man's name, and after that he often went to the palace to visit her.

A little later, the queen made Walter a knight. His full name was then Sir Walter Raleigh.

译文

沃特·罗利爵士（1）

英格兰曾经有一位女王，大家都称她为“好女王贝丝”。

她努力让她的子民生活幸福，子民们也对她敬爱有加。

有一位年轻人听说了女王许多行善的事迹，便来到她的宫殿拜见她。

在他去宫殿的路上，他在一处泥泞的地方遇到了一个女人。这个女人，正是女王陛下。

年轻人马上脱下他身上的天鹅绒斗篷，把它铺在地上，好让女王能走在上面。女王踏着斗篷走过了泥泞，如此一来，她的漂亮鞋子没有沾上一丁点的泥土。

这个年轻人叫沃特，对于他刚才的表现，女王感到很满意。从这以后，沃特就常常能进宫去拜见女王了。

过了一阵子，女王赐封沃特为骑士，沃特的全名也就变成了沃特·罗利爵士。

Sir Walter Raleigh(2)

预习

America /əˈmerɪkə/ 美国

born /bɔːrn/ 出生

dare /der/ 胆敢

Indian /ˈɪndiən/ 印第安人

servant /ˈsɜːrvənt/ 仆人

shut /ʃʌt/ 关上

tobacco /təˈbækoʊ/ 烟草

tower /ˈtaʊər/ 塔

Far over the sea from England, men had found a new country. They gave it the name America.

Few persons knew much about America in those days, and no white men lived there.

Sir Walter Raleigh wished to know a great deal about the new country. He asked the queen to let him have some of the land in America for his own. The queen gladly gave him all that he asked for.

Raleigh named his part of the country Virginia, and sent ships to find out about it. He then sent more than a hundred persons to live in Virginia.

The ships sailed to Virginia, and carried back to England many odd things. Among these were Indian corn and tobacco. The people of England had never seen them before.

Raleigh smoked some of the tobacco. When his servant came in and saw the smoke, he feared that Raleigh was burning up. Then the servant ran and got a pail of water, and dashed it all over Raleigh.

For a time all went well with the people that Raleigh had sent to America. A little white baby was born there. She was named Virginia Dare. She was the first white child born in America.

When the ships came to America again, not one of Raleigh's people could be found. What had happened to them no man knows.

Raleigh then tried to send more persons to Virginia. This he could not do, for the queen died, and she had been Sir Walter's best friend.

After Queen Bess was dead, James became the king of England. The new king did not like Raleigh, and so shut him up in a great tower.

In America there is now a city called Raleigh. It is named for Sir Walter.

译文

沃特·罗利爵士（2）

在海的另一边，在一个离英格兰很远很远的地方，人们发现了一块新的大陆，并给它取名叫“美洲”。

当时，没多少人了解美洲，也没有白人在那里居住。

沃特·罗利爵士渴望了解更多新大陆的事情，他请求女王赐给他一些美洲的土地。女王非常乐意，满足了他的请求。

罗利把他的土地命名为弗吉尼亚，派了许多船只前去开发这片土地。随后，他又派了一百多个人去弗吉尼亚长驻。

他派的船到了弗吉尼亚，返航时就把许多稀奇的玩意儿带回了英格兰。其中，就有印第安人的玉米和烟叶。英格兰的人民以前从来没见过这样的东西。

罗利点燃一撮烟叶，吸了一口，他的仆人刚巧进来，看到烟雾，以为罗利身上着火了。他吓坏了，马上跑出去提了一桶水回来，猛地一浇，把罗利全身浇了个透。

有段时间，罗利派去的人在美国过得不错。一个白人小女孩在那里出生了。她的名字叫弗吉尼亚·戴尔，是第一个在美洲出生的白人。

当航船再度回到美洲时，罗利派去的人全都不见了。他们到底出了什么事，没有人知道。

随后，罗利想派另外的人去弗吉尼亚，但他不能这样做。因为他最好的朋友——贝丝女王去世了。

在贝丝女王过世之后，詹姆斯登基成了英格兰的国王。这位新国王并不喜欢罗利，就把他关进了一座巨塔。

美国，如今有一个名叫“罗利”的城市，它就是以沃特·罗利爵士命名的。

练习

1.填空：

星期一（Monday），星期二（Tuesday），星期三（Wednesday），星期四（Thursday），和星期五（Friday）的时候，我去上学。

星期六（Saturday）的时候，我在玩耍。

星期天（Sunday）的时候，我在休息。

______，______，______，______，______，______，______，加在一起就是一个星期。

2. 星期之中的每一天都有自己对应的英语单词，它们的首字母分别是什么呢？

Robert Bruce

Six times King Robert Bruce had gone into battle at the head of his army. Six times he had lost the battle.

His soldiers were brave and strong, but his army was not large enough. The king that he had to fight had a much larger army.

After the last of these battles, the king hid away in a small house in the woods. Early one morning he was thinking of all that had happened. "I do not know what to do," he said to himself. "I fear that I shall have to give up my country and go away across the sea."

Just then he saw a little spider making a web. She had spun a long fine thread, and now she hung at the end of it. Six times she tried to swing this thread to the next beam, but every time she failed.

"That is just as often as I have tried," said Bruce. "If the spider tries again, and does not fail, I shall try again."

The spider did try again. This time the thread swung to the right place and stayed there.

Bruce was glad. He left the house in the woods, and began to bring his army together. Then they marched again to fight the other king.

The seventh time Robert Bruce and his soldier did not

fail. They won the battle, and the other king and his army had to go back to their own country.

So a tiny spider had helped a king.

(Walter Scott, adapted)

译文

罗伯特 · 布鲁斯

布鲁斯国王曾六次率领军队打仗，但是六次都以失败而告终。

他的士兵们勇敢而坚强，但是他的军队却不够强大，因为他们面临的是一支比他们更强的军队。

在最后一次战斗之后，国王躲在树林的一间小屋子里。一天清晨，他正回首前尘往事的时候自语道："我不知道该怎么办了，我恐怕要放弃我的国家，远渡重洋，离开这里。"

就在这时，他看见一只小蜘蛛正在结网，她纺出了一根长长的细丝，想把细丝挂到下一根横梁上。她试了六次，但是每一次都失败了。

"赶得上我打仗的次数了。"布鲁斯说道，"如果这只蜘蛛第七次没有失败的话，我就也再试一次。"

蜘蛛真的又试了一次，这次她把那根细丝抛上了横梁，稳稳地挂在了那里。

布鲁斯很高兴。他走出了森林里的小屋子，集结军队，又一次踏上征程，去讨伐另一位国王。

这一次，罗伯特 · 布鲁斯和他部下没有失败，他们赢得了这场战斗，把另一个国王和他的军队赶回了他们自己的国家。

就这样，一只小小的蜘蛛帮助了国王。

（沃尔特 · 斯科特爵士，有删改）

The Boys, the Bees, and the British

More than a hundred years ago, there was a great war in our land. King George had sent his soldiers from England to fight our soldiers.

The king's army was called the British army, and was very strong. His soldiers had won many battles.

But the people of our land were very brave, and were not afraid to fight the king's army. Nearly all the men and big boys went to the war as good American soldiers.

In North Carolina a boy, who was only twelve years old, was one day plowing in a field. His father had gone to the war, and the boy was working to help his mother.

All at once this boy heard a great clatter. He looked down the road, and there he saw an army of British soldiers coming. The boy left the horse and plow in the field, and ran to the house.

"Run!" he cried. "Run! The British are coming! Here they come right down the road."

The women ran to the woods to hide. There were only twelve men and boys at home, but they all brought out guns and got ready to fight.

There were four hundred of the British Soon they came up, and began to rob the houses. They took everything that there was to eat. They took even the beds and chairs.

They carried off the corn, and bean to drive away the cows, pigs and chickens.

But just then a queer army came to help the Americans. Somebody upset a beehive. Out came the queen bee and all her army, Buzz! Buzz! Buzz! Who upset that hive? She had never been so angry before in her life.

The bees flew at the British soldiers. Buzz! Buzz! Buzz! Sting! Sting! Sting! The Americans fired their guns, and the British began to run.

More bees came out-of the other hives to help, and the British had to run faster. Soon they were out of sight. And that is how twelve Americans with the help of the bees put to flight four hundred British soldiers.

(Lutie Andrews McCorkle)

译文

男孩、蜜蜂和英国人

一百多年前，美国发生了一场大战。乔治国王从英国派来军队同美国的士兵作战。

国王的战队被称为英国陆军，这支队伍非常强大，队里的士兵曾在很多场战役中取得胜利。

但美国的人民也非常勇敢，面对英国国王的军队毫不畏惧。几乎全国的成年男性和年龄稍大的男孩都加入军队，参加了这场战役。

在北卡罗莱纳州有一个小男孩，刚满十二岁。一天，这个小男孩在农田耕作，他的爸爸去参战了，所以小男孩得帮妈妈干活。

突然，小男孩听到了一阵很大的“咔哒”声。他低头朝公路望过去，结果发现一队英国士兵正在走过来。小男孩立马把马和犁丢在农田，朝家里跑过去。

“快跑！”他大叫道，“快跑呀！英国人来了！他们正在沿着这条路开过来呢。”

女人们赶紧跑向树林躲了起来。整个村落只有十二个男人和男孩还在家，但他们全部都拿出了枪，做好了战斗的准备。

英国这边共有四百名士兵，很快就到了。他们一到这里，就开始进屋抢劫。他们抢走了百姓屋里所有的食物，甚至把床和椅子也抢走了。

他们又抢走了玉米和豆子来驱赶牛、猪和鸡这些牲畜、家禽。

但就在这时，一支奇怪的军队忽然登场了，这支队伍是来帮助美国人的。有人把蜂箱打翻了。于是，蜂后带着她的战队出现了：“嗡！

嗡！嗡！”究竟是谁打翻了蜂箱？蜂后这辈子还从没这么生气过！

这些蜜蜂扑向了英国士兵。“嗡！嗡！嗡！叮！叮！叮！”美国人也趁机开火了，不堪忍受攻击的英国人开始四处逃窜。

这时，其他蜂箱的蜜蜂也出来帮忙了，英国人不得不加快逃跑的速度。很快，他们就跑得不见踪影了。这就是十二个美国人在蜜蜂的帮助下，击退四百个英国士兵的故事。

（卢蒂亚 · 安德鲁斯 · 麦克科尔）

《美国语文》译者名录

钱志慧	南京师范大学
帕孜丽娅	暨南大学
尹吴娅琪	中南财经政法大学
侯艺东	南京师范大学
夏婕	南方医科大学
金晓寒	复旦大学
张佳佳	南京林业大学
杜子悦	华中师范大学
高倩	华东师范大学
蒋荟蓉	西南交通大学
赵艺珂	南开大学
苌婧	四川外国语大学
李颖	北京外国语大学

美工

彭慧	华东师范大学